DRUG TRANSIT AND DISTRIBUTION, INTERCEPTION AND CONTROL

NARCOTICS DECRIMINALIZATION

ADOPTED PRACTICES IN SELECT COUNTRIES

DRUG TRANSIT AND DISTRIBUTION, INTERCEPTION AND CONTROL

Additional books in this series can be found on Nova's website under the Series tab.

Additional e-books in this series can be found on Nova's website under the e-book tab.

DRUG TRANSIT AND DISTRIBUTION, INTERCEPTION AND CONTROL

NARCOTICS DECRIMINALIZATION

ADOPTED PRACTICES IN SELECT COUNTRIES

DENISE TORRES
EDITOR

NOVINKA

New York

NOTICE TO THE READER

Library of Congress Cataloging-in-Publication Data

ISBN: 978-1-53610-318-2

Published by Nova Science Publishers, Inc. † New York

CONTENTS

Preface		**vii**
Chapter 1	Decriminalization of Narcotics *Law Library of Congress, Global Legal Research Center*	**1**
Chapter 2	Marijuana: Medical and Retail—Selected Legal Issues *Todd Garvey, Charles Doyle and David H. Carpenter*	**93**
Related Nova Publication		**127**
Index		**129**

PREFACE

This book, prepared by the foreign law specialists and analysts of the Law Library of Congress, provides a review of laws adopted in Argentina, Australia, Brazil, Canada, Costa Rica, the Czech Republic, Germany, Ireland, Israel, Mexico, the Netherlands, New Zealand, Norway, Portugal, South Africa, and Uruguay with regard to legalization, decriminalization, or other forms of regulation of narcotics and other psychoactive substances. Individual country surveys included in this study demonstrate varied approaches to the problem of prosecuting drug use, possession, manufacturing, purchase, and sale. Furthermore, the book discusses medical and retail-selected legal issues of marijuana.

In: Narcotics Decriminalization
Editor: Denise Torres
ISBN: 978-1-53610-318-2

Chapter 1

DECRIMINALIZATION OF NARCOTICS*

Law Library of Congress, Global Legal Research Center

COMPARATIVE SUMMARY

Peter Roudik
Director of Legal Research

This report, prepared by the foreign law specialists and analysts of the Law Library of Congress, provides a review of laws adopted in Argentina, Australia, Brazil, Canada, Costa Rica, the Czech Republic, Germany, Ireland, Israel, Mexico, the Netherlands, New Zealand, Norway, Portugal, South Africa, and Uruguay with regard to legalization, decriminalization, or other forms of regulation of narcotics and other psychoactive substances. Individual country surveys included in this study demonstrate varied approaches to the problem of prosecuting drug use, possession, manufacturing, purchase, and sale.

The country surveys demonstrate some diversity and common threads among these jurisdictions as to defining narcotics, distinguishing between "hard" and "soft" drugs, establishing special regulations

* This is an edited, reformatted and augmented version of a report issued by the Law Library of Congress, Global Legal Research Center, July 2016.

concerning cannabis, refusing to prosecute personal use and/or possession of small quantities of drugs for personal use, giving law enforcement authorities the discretion not to prosecute minors and first-time offenders, applying alternative forms of punishment, and providing treatment opportunities. The following approaches toward decriminalization of narcotics were identified:

- Production, marketing, and consumption of marijuana is legalized and regulated (Uruguay);
- Drugs are prohibited but the sale and use of soft drugs is tolerated and regulated (Netherlands);
- The personal possession and use of small amounts of drugs is not penalized while other drug-related activities are prohibited (Costa Rica, Czech Republic, Mexico, Portugal); and
- Treatment and alternative punishments for minor drug offenses are allowed (Argentina, Australia, Brazil, Germany, Israel, New Zealand, Norway).

While most of the countries reviewed do not prosecute individual drug users or have an option for avoiding their criminal prosecution, in general, possessing, manufacturing, and trading in drugs is prohibited. The Czech Republic made the possession of drugs legal after the collapse of the Communist regime but reinstated the penalties for possession in "larger than small" amounts shortly thereafter.

Most of the countries differentiate between soft and hard drugs, listing cannabis as a soft narcotic, and two countries, the Netherlands and Uruguay, provide for special cannabis-related rules. While in the Netherlands marijuana is still classified as an illicit substance, these two countries tolerate and regulate the use of cannabis. Other jurisdictions provide for less strict or suspended punishment, or substitute traditional punishment with voluntary addiction treatment, community work, or other forms of alternative punishment if someone is caught using or dealing soft drugs. Additionally, New Zealand regulates the production and sale of so-called "new psychoactive substances," such as party pills and synthetic cannabis. Previously unregulated and sold without restrictions, these drugs recently became subject to government control, including the regulation of their sale. In Germany, even though drugs are divided into different schedules, for law enforcement purposes all narcotics are treated equally, and the distinction between soft and hard drugs can only be considered at sentencing, taking into account associated risks and damages.

In all of the countries reviewed such drug-related offenses as distributing drugs, possessing them in large amounts, cultivating plants containing a narcotic substance, producing drugs and possessing items for their production, etc., are recognized as crimes. Meanwhile, the possession of drugs for personal use in small amounts is no longer a criminal offense in some jurisdictions, but rather a misdemeanor subject to a monetary fine or other nonpecuniary punishment. These jurisdictions include Brazil, the Czech Republic, Norway, Portugal, and the Australian Capital Territory. An interesting example is provided by Costa Rica where the use of narcotics, including personal use, is prohibited by law but no penalty for this violation is found in the Criminal Code. In Argentina, the possession of narcotics remains illegal but the Supreme Court has ruled that "private actions of individuals are exempt from the authority of judges as long as they do not offend or injure others," declaring penalties against an adult who consumed marijuana unconstitutional.

Costa Rica, Germany, Israel, New Zealand, and the Australian State of New South Wales are among those jurisdictions where the police, prosecutors, or courts have discretion to drop charges if a minor offense involving prohibited drugs has been committed for the first time and the accused person is willing to undergo addiction treatment.

The possession and use of narcotics is a crime under the laws of most of the countries included in this report. However, in some countries medical treatment is prescribed for those found in violation of drug laws or can be chosen by the accused person as an alternative to traditional punishment. Mexican law requires that individuals found in possession of limited quantities of narcotics be referred to addiction treatment programs. In Norway a minor drug offender can opt to enroll in a drug treatment program instead of going to prison, but violation of the treatment program conditions will place the offender in jail. In Argentina a judge may replace imprisonment by detoxification and rehabilitation treatment. Special treatment for children is prescribed by the laws of New Zealand.

It appears that where decriminalization of drug-related activities has occurred, it was done with the purpose of securing the health and safety of the individual and the public. Even in those countries where the use of some drugs is allowed (Uruguay), advertising or promoting drugs, or consuming them in a public place, is prohibited. Dutch legislation emphasizes that coffee shops are prohibited from advertising drugs and causing a nuisance. The reduction of harm from drug use is the declared purpose for the creation of varied medical and social service facilities (e.g., needle exchanges, drug consumption rooms). However, even the authorization of such services by law (Germany, Netherlands, Portugal) has not resulted in the legalization of narcotics.

Information on pending proposals for the legalization of cannabis in Canada and South Africa, and decriminalization of the possession of small amounts of heroin, cocaine, and cannabis for personal use in Ireland, is also included in the report.

COUNTRIES WHERE CANNABIS IS LEGAL AND REGULATED

URUGUAY

Graciela Rodriguez-Ferrand
Senior Foreign Law Specialist

Summary

Uruguay's Law to Legalize and Regulate Cannabis adopted in 2013 brought radical change to the country's approach to cannabis production and use. The law allows legal access to marijuana in four ways: medical marijuana through the Ministry of Health, home-grown marijuana, membership clubs, and sales to adults in drugstores. Although registration of consumers and cannabis clubs has been completed, implementation of sales in pharmacies is still underway. The law provides for education and public health awareness as to the risks involved in the consumption of marijuana.

I. Introduction

By adopting Law No. 19172 on December 20, 2013,[1] Uruguay became the first country in Latin America to legalize and regulate cannabis.[2] The aim of the law is to prevent abusive consumption of marijuana and educate the population about its harmful effects, while combating drug trafficking.[3] The law regulates the production, marketing, and consumption of cannabis, while promoting education about and prevention of cannabis use.[4]

When introducing the bill in the Senate, the congressional majority report laid out the basis of the measure as an alternative to policies of prohibition as well as a regulation of the market of drugs in order to give the government a more efficient way to reduce supply and demand.[5] The congressional debate was centered on three main issues: an increase in marijuana consumption, its harmful effects on health and the difficulties to supervise and monitor compliance with the law.[6]

II. Cannabis Regulation

Under the new law, the state controls the cannabis industry chain, from production to consumption, including the import, export, planting, cultivation, harvesting, acquisition, storage, marketing, and distribution of cannabis and its derivatives, through the institutions empowered by law.[7]

Law 19172 created the Institute for the Regulation and Control of Cannabis (IRCC) to regulate the planting, cultivation, harvesting, production, processing, storage, distribution, and sale of cannabis.[8] The IRCC also promotes and proposes actions to reduce risks and harms derived from cannabis use and monitors compliance with the law.[9] The National Council on Drugs (NCD), created in 1988,[10] is the authority that sets the national policy on cannabis in accordance with the objectives of Law 19172, with the cooperation and advice of the IRCC.[11]

Although amended many times, Decree-Law 14294[12] of 1974 is still in force with regard to all drugs except for cannabis. As to those other drugs, Decree-Law 14294 allows consumption, but penalizes possession for purposes other than consumption.[13]

Law 19172 provides that the planting, growing, harvesting, and marketing of cannabis must be authorized by the IRCC.[14] The authority of the IRCC includes issuing licenses to produce, process, collect, distribute, and sell industrial and psychoactive cannabis; registering users and those engaged in self-cultivation; authorizing cannabis club membership; monitoring compliance with the law; determining and adjudicating sanctions for violations; and enforcing the imposition of sanctions.[15]

Sanctions for violations of Law 19172 include warnings, fines, confiscation of goods or items, destruction of goods, suspension of the offender in the pertinent registry, temporary or permanent disqualification from transacting in cannabis, and partial or complete closure of establishments.[16]

Law 19172 amended article 30 of Decree-Law 14294 to provide that the production without legal authorization of raw materials or substances capable of producing psychological or physical dependency is subject to a prison sentence of twenty months to ten years, except when produced for scientific or pharmaceutical research, or for medicinal use.[17] However, the production of marijuana by planting, growing, and harvesting cannabis plants with psychoactive effects when meeting legal requirements under the law does not give rise to criminal liability.[18]

Law 19172 decriminalizes anyone who possesses psychoactive cannabis plants in a reasonable quantity, exclusively for his or her personal consumption.[19] The maximum quantity considered for personal use is 40 grams.[20] It further provides that anyone who keeps, holds, stores, or possesses in his/her home a harvest of up to six cannabis plants with psychoactive effects or a harvest obtained through membership in a cannabis club that results in a maximum of 480 grams will not be subject to criminal penalties.[21] Home growers of marijuana are required to register in the IRCC and are not permitted to register more than one domicile for this purpose.[22] Any unauthorized cannabis patch must be eradicated upon a court's order.[23]

Cannabis clubs are duly registered civil entities of between fifteen and forty-five members that are allowed to grow up to ninety-nine marijuana plants in specific places.[24] No member may access more than 480 grams a year.[25] Marijuana membership clubs that plant, cultivate, and harvest psychoactive cannabis for personal or shared domestic consumption are subject to the control of the IRCC, and must be authorized by the Ministry of Education and Culture.[26]

Only Uruguayan nationals or foreigners with legal residence in the country who have reached the age of majority (eighteen years of age), and are not incapacitated may become members of these clubs.[27] Both the clubs and their members must be registered in the Cannabis Registry within the IRCC.[28] Identity information entered into the Cannabis Registry will be considered sensitive and protected.[29] Registration of cultivation is free of charge for the petitioners.[30]

The IRCC also has the authority to issue licenses for the sale of psychoactive cannabis to pharmacies.[31] Marijuana to be sold in drugstores will be produced by a limited number of companies previously selected through national and international bidding.[32] The legal sale of cannabis by pharmacies is expected to begin in July 2016.[33] Fifty pharmacies have registered with the IRCC and the Ministry of Public Health since May 2016, when the government opened the registry.[34] Registered pharmacies are required to install fingerprint recognition software to identify consumers and safety boxes to protect the marijuana in stock.[35] Registered consumers will be allowed to purchase 10 grams per week or 40 grams per month.[36] The government faces the difficult task of communicating that people should buy marijuana only through approved channels like pharmacies or clubs while avoiding encouraging its consumption.[37]

According to pharmacy associations, the low number of pharmacies registered is due to concerns that the sale of marijuana would affect their image with regard to clients with traditional values, especially in provinces where the population is against the legal sale of cannabis.[38]

III. Public Health, Education, and Social Safeguards

Law 19172 provides for the National Integrated Health System (NIHS) to take measures aimed at education, awareness campaigns, and prevention with regard to the health risks of cannabis use, particularly addiction.[39] The National Public Education System is required to set up educational policies aimed at the promotion of health and the prevention of harmful cannabis use at the elementary, secondary, and vocational education levels.[40]

Advertising or promoting cannabis in any way and consumption of cannabis in public spaces is prohibited.[41] Similarly, those eighteen years old or younger and those who are legally incapacitated will not have access to cannabis for recreational use.[42] Driving under the influence of cannabis will be sanctioned with disqualification from driving if the concentration found in the driver's body is beyond the allowable amount.[43]

IV. Legislative and Political Debate

In 2011 grassroots activists started a movement for some form of regulation of the use of marijuana for personal consumption.[44] The Comisión de Adicciones de Diputados (Commission on Addictions of the Chamber of Deputies in Congress) gathered all the stakeholders on this issue, including doctors, educators, politicians, law enforcement, students, etc., to debate the different approaches and solutions to marijuana consumption.[45]

According to a report by the National Council on Drugs, the debate was prompted by the failure of prohibition and the increase in marijuana consumption by youth.[46] The debate was extensive, which allowed the Uruguayan society to be informed on the issues at stake.[47] Each aspect of the law was subject to comprehensive debate.[48] The government's goal was to reach consensus on a legal framework directed at reducing profits for the illegal cannabis market while raising awareness of the public health consequences and harmful effects of marijuana consumption.[49]

The government aimed at establishing legal mechanisms to access cannabis, specifying the amount allowed to be grown for individual consumption.[50] The government sought to give legality to the marijuana market by managing it, while at the same time obtaining resources to fund support and treatment programs for drug addictions and to conduct prevention campaigns.[51]

The media and polling entities played a key role in the success of this debate by reaching out to all sectors of society, from families to activist groups.[52] The end product was a law that will regulate the marijuana market to protect the users and their health while depriving criminal organizations of their share of the marijuana market.[53]

Countries that Do Not Penalize Personal Possession and Use

Costa Rica

Norma C. Gutiérrez
Senior Foreign Law Specialist

Summary

The General Health Law of Costa Rica prohibits the personal use of narcotics and other drugs, but does not penalize those who violate this prohibition. Likewise, Law No. 8204 on Narcotics and Psychotropic Substances, Unauthorized Drugs, Related Activities, Money Laundering and the Financing of Terrorism penalizes all activities related to the production, commerce, and trafficking of such narcotics and substances, but does not punish their personal consumption. Prior Law No. 7093 of 1988 also did not prohibit or penalize the personal use of illegal drugs. However, a comprehensive amendment promulgated by Law No. 7233 of 1991 imposed fines for the consumption of unauthorized drugs in public places. Both Law No. 7093 and 7233 were superseded by the current Law No. 8204.

A bill that would regulate the production of cannabis and hemp plants for medical and industrial purposes was debated in the Legislative Assembly in December of 2014 However, that bill has yet to pass. In January 2016 a criminal tribunal in the city of Alajuela acquitted an attorney who had planted marijuana for personal consumption.

I. Introduction

Controlled substances are governed in Costa Rica by the General Health Law[1] and Law No. 8204 on Narcotics (*estupefacientes*) and Psychotropic Substances, Unauthorized Drugs, Related Activities, Money Laundering and the Financing of Terrorism.[2] Neither of them punish the personal use of unauthorized drugs, as explained below.

II. General Health Law

Article 28 of the General Health Law prohibits the "personal use" of narcotics, and of tranquilizers, stimulants, and hallucinogens that are subject to restricted use under international conventions and by the laws of the country, with the exception of their use for therapeutic reasons and with a medical prescription under the express authorization of the Ministry of Health.[3]

Similarly, article 127 of the General Health Law prohibits the cultivation, import, export, trafficking and use of *papaver somniferum* or poppies, *erythroxylon coca* or coca, *cannabis indica* and *cannabis sativa* or cannabis, and all plants and seeds of similar effects that are so declared by the Ministry of Health, and mandates their destruction.[4]

Although article 28 of the General Health Law specifically prohibits the personal use of narcotics and other drugs, no penalty for its violation is found in the Code. In contrast, under article 371 of the Code, a penalty of six to twelve years' imprisonment may be imposed on those who, for whatever reason, grow poppies, coca, cannabis, or plants of similar effect whose cultivation, possession, or trafficking has been prohibited or restricted by the Ministry of Health.[5]

Article 137 of the General Health Law requires the confiscation and destruction of any drug that is illegally cultivated, possessed, traded, distributed, or stored.[6]

III. Statutory Law on Narcotics and Psychotropic Substances

While superseded Law No. 7093 on Narcotics and Psychotropic Substances penalized with eight to twenty years' imprisonment the illegal cultivation, manufacture, preparation, refining, transport, distribution, storage, and trafficking of drugs and their financing,[7] it did not prohibit or impose penalties for the personal use of illegal drugs.

Law No. 7093 was considerably amended by Law No. 7233 of 1991.[8] Although the amended Law 7093 did not impose penalties restricting the personal freedom of the drug user for his/her personal use of drugs, it penalized this activity with fines. Article 24 imposed sixty- to 180-dayfines on persons who consumed or used unauthorized drugs in public places or in public places. If the person was a minor, the appropriate authorities had to inform the minor's parents or guardian.[9]

Law No. 7093 was superseded by the current Law No. 8204 on Narcotics and Psychotropic Substances, Unauthorized Drugs, Related Activities, Money Laundering and the Financing of Terrorism, effective January 11, 2002, which regulates narcotics (*estupefacientes*), psychotropic substances, and drugs likely to cause physical or psychological dependencies.[10] Law No. 8204 contains no provision penalizing the personal use of unauthorized drugs, but imposes the penalty of imprisonment for other drug-related activities, such as cultivation, production, manufacture, refining, preparation, distribution, commerce, supply, transport, and storage of the drugs and substances regulated by the Law.[11]

Moreover, article 79 of Law No. 8204 mandates the promotion and facilitation of free, voluntary placement or outpatient treatment for therapy and rehabilitation in public or private health centers to persons who use unauthorized drugs on the streets or in public places. If the drug users are minors, the authorities are obliged to inform the National Child Welfare Agency (Patronato Nacional de la Infancia, PANI) of the situation, and PANI will mandate compulsory treatment.[12]

In 2010 the Office of the Public Prosecutor issued a guideline, Instructivo General No. 02-2010, stating that under article 28 of the Constitution, no one may be disturbed or prosecuted for any act that does not infringe the law. The guideline also invokes article 39 of the Constitution, stating that one will be made to suffer a penalty except for a crime, offense, or fault sanctioned by a previous law. Based on these constitutional provisions, the guideline instructs court prosecutors to reject police reports of possession of drugs for personal use.[13] Another guideline, Instrucción General 01/2011, instructs prosecutors to assess police reports of confiscated unauthorized drugs, to remit the drugs for destruction, and to order the immediate release of the detainee when the case is not connected to any criminal activity; otherwise, criminal proceedings will be initiated.[14]

Law No. 9161 added article 77*bis* to Law No. 8204, imposing a penalty of three to eight years' imprisonment, rather than the longer term of eight to twenty years imposed by article 77, on a woman who brings narcotics or psychotropic substances into a prison if the following circumstances are met: the woman is in poverty; the woman is the head of a household in vulnerable conditions; the woman has under her care minors, elderly people, or people with any disability; or the woman is elderly in conditions of vulnerability. The judge, after finding that any of the above circumstances are present, may order that the penalty be served by house arrest or probation.[15]

IV. Recent Developments

A. Proposed Legislation

In 2014 a bill to regulate the use of cannabis for therapeutic purposes, the Draft Law on Research, Regulation, and Control of Cannabis and Hemp Plants for Medical, Food, and Industrial Uses, was submitted to the Legislative Assembly.[16] Although the bill was initially debated during an extraordinary session of the Legislative Assembly in December of 2014,[17] it has not yet been approved.[18]

B. Criminal Tribunal Ruling

According to a report in *La Nación*, a criminal tribunal in Alajuela, the second most important Costa Rican city and the capital of the province of the same name, has acquitted a lawyer who was arrested four times for growing marijuana for personal consumption. After the verdict, the accused person's attorneys explained that growing marijuana in someone's home for personal consumption carries no criminal penalties or economic sanctions. Article 58 of Law No. 8204 penalizes with eight to fifteen years' imprisonment anyone who "without authorization distributes, trades, supplies, manufactures, develops, refines, transforms, extracts, prepares, cultivates, produces, transports, stores or sales drugs or cultivates the plants from which such substances are obtained," they said, but article 58 does not penalize the personal consumption of drugs. In addition, they argued that the only thing that the authorities can do if they find crops of drugs for personal use is to confiscate and destroy them, as required by article 137 of the General Health Law.[19]

The tribunal's decision was based on the fact that it could not be proved that the drugs were destined for sale and trafficking. The judge explained that, although growing marijuana is in fact illegal, it is not a crime if it is not sold.

Moreover, the judge added that if the attorney continued growing marijuana, the appropriate authorities would continue confiscating it.

The fifty-six-year-old lawyer, who had been arrested four times for the same charges of growing marijuana in his home located thirty meters from the tribunal, was facing twenty-four years of imprisonment. The tribunal's ruling was a two-to-one decision of a three-judge panel. The dissenting judge argued that he reached the conclusion that with the number of plants the defendant had planted, he could have manufactured 5,000 marijuana cigarettes.[20]

Czech Republic

Nerses Isajanyan
Foreign Law Consultant

Summary

The Czech Republic is the only Eastern European country in the post-Communist era to have reduced punishments for some drug-related activities. The production and sale of drugs have always been punishable under Czech criminal law. The possession of drugs was decriminalized after the collapse of the Communist regime, but penalties were reinstated in 1999 for possession in amounts "larger than small." The new Criminal Code enacted in 2009 differentiates between cannabis and other drugs, and imposes less strict penalties for the use and cultivation of cannabis. The use of cannabis for medical purposes was legalized in 2013.

Despite inheriting from the Soviet bloc a policy of harshly repressing drug users, today the Czech Republic has a drug policy that is described as "pragmatic, rational and sometimes too liberal."[1]

The 1961 Criminal Law was the main piece of legislation on drug-related offenses until 2010, when the new Criminal Code came into effect.[2] Articles 187 and 188 of the 1961 Law criminalized the possession, production, and sale of narcotic substances.[3] After the collapse of the Communist regime, the possession of drugs for personal use was decriminalized in 1990.[4] Instead, a new crime, "spreading addiction," was included in the Criminal Law. In 1999, a new section 187a was added to the Criminal Law that made it a crime to possess drugs in amounts "larger than small."[5]

In 2009, the Czech Republic enacted a new Criminal Code that repealed the Criminal Law of 1961.[6] The new Code established penalties of six months to five years of imprisonment for producing and distributing drugs,[7] possessing them "in an amount larger than small,"[8] cultivating plants containing a narcotic substance,[9] producing drugs and possessing items for their production,[10] spreading drug addiction,[11] and producing substances with hormonal effects.[12] The sections in the Criminal Code on possession for personal use and the cultivation of plants treat cannabis differently from other drugs and provide for less strict penalties.[13]

The possession of drugs for personal use in small amounts is not a criminal offense, but rather a misdemeanor subject to a monetary fine of up to 15,000 Czech koruna (approximately US$612).[14] A major issue in drug enforcement since 1999 has been that of determining what constitutes a "small amount" of drugs. Initially, this was decided on a case-by-case basis within the judicial system.[15] However, in 2009, the government issued a resolution specifying the "small amounts" for various drugs.[16] This resolution, however, was abolished in 2013 by the Constitutional Court, which found that only a law, not a government regulation, could define what constitutes a criminal offense.[17] Subsequently, the definition of "small amounts" was clarified in an opinion of the Criminal Division of the Supreme Court, which mostly duplicated the government's resolution, but set stricter rules for the most common drugs.[18] In particular, the Supreme Court decriminalized the possession of 1.5 g of methamphetamine, 1.5 g of heroin, 1 g of cocaine, 10 g of cannabis dry matter, 5 units of ecstasy, and 5 g of hashish.[19] The Court also stated that "the drug user's possession of only one dose before using it is not illegal possession."[20]

In November 2013 the police arrested a number of "growshop" owners after the Supreme Court held that the combined selling of cannabis seeds, fertilizers, flowerpots, and books for cannabis cultivation fulfilled the elements of the crime of spreading drug addiction.[21] According to the police, these shops promoted drug use by offering the complete technology needed for cannabis cultivation.[22]

Those who cultivate cannabis for personal use may find the application of the various provisions of the Criminal Code confusing.[23] For example, a person caught growing cannabis plants may be subject to penalties for cultivation,[24] but if the arrest occurs after harvesting and during the process of drying, the offense is qualified as production,[25] and if the plants have already been dried, the person is charged with illegal possession.[26]

Cannabis for medical use was allowed by law in 2013.[27] An implementing regulation allows for prescription of 180 g of dry matter per month.[28] There is a special electronic prescription form, and only specialized medical professionals are permitted to prescribe cannabis, not general practitioners.[29] Growing or importing medical cannabis is subject to licensing.[30]

MEXICO

Gustavo Guerra
Senior Foreign Law Specialist

I. Relevant Law

Although possession of illegal drugs is generally a crime under Mexican law, possession of the following narcotics is not criminally punishable in amounts that do not exceed the listed quantities. Such small amounts of narcotics are considered by law to be for immediate and personal consumption, which is not criminally punishable, provided that such possession takes place outside of certain places, including educational institutions and prisons:

Narcotic	Maximum Amount for Immediate and Personal Consumption	
Opium	2 g	
Heroin or diacetylmorphine	50 mg	
Cannabis	5 g	
Cocaine	500 mg	
LSD	0.015 mg	
MDA, Methylenedioxyamphetamine	*Powder*	*Capsules or tablets*
	40 mg	1 unit whose weight is not higher than 200 mg
MDMA, 3,4-Methylenedioxymethamphetamine	40 mg	1 unit whose weight is not higher than 200 mg
Methamphetamines	40 mg	1 unit whose weight is not higher than 200 mg[1]

Source: From article 479 of the Ley General de Salud, infra note 1, as translated by the author.

Individuals who are found in possession of these narcotics in quantities at or below the listed amounts must be referred to addiction treatment programs.[2]

This rule was enacted in 2009 pursuant to an initiative introduced in 2008, which indicated that the list of drugs and quantities the possession of which is not criminally punishable was compiled based on information provided by law enforcement and health authorities concerning the most commonly consumed drugs in Mexico.[3] The policy underlying the initiative was that consumers of drugs should be treated not as criminals but as persons suffering from addiction, which should be treated as a public-health problem rather than as a crime.[4]

II. Initiative on Legalizing Medical Use of Cannabis

In June 2016, Mexico's Senate announced that it is considering an initiative to legalize the medicinal use of cannabis.[5] This initiative proposes to grant authority to Mexico's Department of Health to design and execute policies aimed at regulating the production and use of medicinal products derived from cannabis, as well as the importation of cannabis-based medicines from abroad.[6] It is unclear whether this initiative will become law.

NETHERLANDS

Jenny Gesley
Foreign Law Specialist

Summary

The Dutch Opium Act contains the legal rules pertaining to narcotics. The Act differentiates between soft and hard drugs. In general, possession and trade in drugs is illegal, but penalties are more severe for hard drugs. The Prosecutor-General publishes directives that set out the Dutch tolerance policy in drug cases, which means that even though the activity is technically illegal, the offender will not be prosecuted as long as certain conditions are met. The directives address the operation of coffee shops in which soft drugs may be purchased and used, the different approaches in cases involving hard drugs and soft drugs, and what constitutes a small quantity of drugs for personal use. Furthermore, courts have the option to suspend the detention of an addict with a history of crime on the condition that he or she undergoes treatment in a special institution for intensive treatment.

I. General Overview

The legal rules concerning narcotic drugs are set out in the Dutch Opium Act.[1] The Opium Act differentiates between "hard drugs" (schedule I) and "soft drugs" (schedule II). Cannabis is listed in schedule II. Sentences for acts involving substances listed in schedule I are more severe than for those listed in schedule II.[2]

"Drugs" include substances and preparations.[3] "Substances" are defined as "elements with a human, animal, plant or chemical origin, including animals, plants, parts of animals or plants, as well as micro-organisms."[4] "Preparations" are defined as "solid or liquid mixtures of substances."[5]

In general, bringing drugs into and taking them out of the territory of the Netherlands, and growing, preparing, treating, processing, selling, supplying, providing, transporting, possessing, and manufacturing drugs, is prohibited in the Netherlands.[6] Exceptions exist for pharmacists, doctors, dentists and veterinary surgeons within the normal practice of their professions.[7] Furthermore, an application for an exemption from the Opium Act for cannabis and cannabis resin can be filed with the Bureau voor Medicinale Cannabis (Office for Medicinal Cannabis Research) for reasons of public health, animal health, academic or chemical analytical research, training, or trade-related purposes.[8]

II. Dutch Drug Policy

The Prosecutor-General issues directives that define the Dutch prosecution policy in drug cases. The directives address, among other issues, the conditions of operating coffee shops, the different approaches in cases involving hard drugs and soft drugs, and what constitutes a small quantity of drugs for personal use.

Technically, it is illegal to buy and sell soft drugs, but the Dutch government tolerates the sale of soft drugs in coffee shops to prevent users of soft drugs from coming into contact with hard drugs.[9] Coffee shops are establishments where cannabis may be sold and used but no alcoholic drinks may be sold or consumed.[10] As long as certain conditions and guidelines are met (discussed below), the public prosecutor's office will not prosecute, under a policy of tolerance (*gedoogbeleid*). In addition, if anyone is caught with small quantities of drugs for personal use outside of a coffee shop, he or she will not be prosecuted.

A. Coffee Shops

The Opium Act Directive[11] sets out the rules for the toleration policy applicable to the operation of coffee shops. Coffee shops are prohibited from

- advertising,
- possessing or selling hard drugs,
- causing a nuisance,
- allowing minors to enter the premises or selling soft drugs to them,
- selling more than a limited amount of soft drugs per transaction and having more than 500 grams in stock, and
- allowing nonresidents of the Netherlands to enter the premises and buy soft drugs.

The rules that the coffee shops need to adhere to are called "AHOJGI-criteria," formed by the initial letters of the Dutch words for the individual criteria.[12] The residency requirement came into effect on January 1, 2013. It was added in order to combat rising drug-related crime and nuisance caused by drug dealers and drug users, in particular users from abroad.[13]

Within the national framework, local governments choose how to implement the criteria. They are also authorized to add additional criteria for the operation of coffee shops.[14] Mayors are in charge of enforcement of the tolerance criteria.[15] If a coffee shop does not adhere to the AHOJGI-criteria, the mayor is authorized to close the business.[16]

Some cities like Amsterdam have chosen not to enforce the Dutch residency requirement in coffee shops, because they generate most of their income from tourists. The mayor of Amsterdam made that decision based on the coalition agreement presented by the new government in October 2012.[17]

The national government also discussed adding a distance requirement from schools to the AHOJGI-criteria, which was supposed to go into effect on January 1, 2014. According to the plan, coffee shops had to be located at least

350 meters away from any schools that had students younger than 18 years.[18] The plan was eventually discarded, but local authorities are free to adopt it nonetheless and most cities have established a distance requirement of 250 meters.[19]

B. User Rooms

Some local authorities have also established so called "user rooms," in which drug addicts may use their own drugs in a clean environment and will not become a nuisance for the public. The establishments are not allowed to provide or sell drugs. In general, social workers are present to offer therapy options. The use of drugs in "user rooms" is also tolerated by the prosecution.[20]

C. Soft Drugs

The Directive for the Prosecution of Opium Act Offenses – Soft Drugs[21] defines a small quantity of soft drugs for personal use as an amount of up to 5 grams. Likewise there is a presumption that the cultivating of no more than five cannabis plants is merely for personal use. Anyone who possesses or trades a small quantity of soft drugs or cultivates less than five plants for personal use will not be prosecuted. The directive states that the offender has to relinquish the drugs and that they will be taken out of circulation.[22] For the possession of larger amounts of soft drugs, first-time offenders incur a fine; offenders who have been caught twice will either incur a fine or community service; and offenders who have committed multiple offenses will either have to pay a fine, do community service, or serve a prison sentence.

D. Hard Drugs

With regard to hard drugs, possession of small quantities of up to 0.5 grams/1 pill for personal use will also not be prosecuted.[23] As with soft drugs, the offender will have to relinquish the drugs and they will be taken out of circulation. The prosecution of possession of larger amounts follows the same principle as the prosecution for possession of soft drugs with the difference that the fines are higher and the community service and prison time is longer.

III. Placement in an Institution for Habitual Offenders

In 2004, the Placement in an Institution for Habitual Offenders Act came into effect.[24] It incorporates the Penal Care Facility for Addicts Act, which was adopted in 2001. The Act provides that addicts with a history of crime or habitual offenders in general may be committed to a special institution for intensive treatment for a period of at most two years. The offender's detention is suspended on the condition that he or she undergoes treatment in such an institution.

PORTUGAL

Eduardo Soares
Senior Foreign Law Specialist

Summary

In 1999, after the approval of a national strategy to combat drugs and drug addiction, the Portuguese government issued Law No. 30/2000, which decriminalized the acquisition, possession, and use of specified plants, substances, or preparations for a person's own consumption, and turned such conduct into misdemeanors. Law No. 30/2000 created a Commission for Drug Dissuasion for the processing of these misdemeanors and the application of sanctions, which is regulated by Decree-Law No. 130-A/2001. To further implement the strategy, the government in 2001 enacted Decree-Law No. 183, which approved a general system of prevention policies, risk reduction, and minimization of harm that created programs and public health structures for increasing awareness and providing for the referral of drug addicts for treatment.

I. Introduction

In the late 1990s, drug addiction was a major concern in Portugal.[1] To address the situation, on February 16, 1998, the government issued an order creating the Commission for the National Strategy for Drug Control (Comissão para a Estratégia Nacional de Combate à Droga), which was charged with proposing a national strategy to combat drugs. That strategy contains the basic guidelines of the policy on drugs and drug addiction in various fields, including primary prevention, treatment, social rehabilitation, training and research, risk reduction, and combatting drug trafficking.[2]

Based on a report prepared by the Commission, on April 22, 1999, the government approved the first National Strategy for the Fight Against Drugs and Drug Addiction (Estratégia Nacional de Luta Contra a Droga e a Toxicodependência) for the period 1999–2004. [3] The Strategy recommended decriminalization of drug use and the reclassification of drug use, possession, and purchase as administrative offenses (*ilícitos de mera ordenação social*).[4] The Strategy noted that maintaining criminal sanctions was justified with regard to the cultivation of drugs for consumption, because cultivation dangerously aligns with trafficking.[5]

To implement the National Strategy, the government enacted Law No. 30 of November 29, 2000; Decree-Law No. 130-A of April 23, 2001; and Decree-Law No. 183 of June 21, 2001 (all discussed below).

II. Law No. 30 of November 29, 2000

The National Strategy led to the approval of Law No. 30 of November 29, 2000, which defines the legal regime applicable to the use of narcotic drugs and psychotropic substances, and the health and social protection of people who consume such substances without a prescription.[6] The plants, substances, and preparations subject to this legal regime are listed in tables I through IV of Decree-Law No. 15 of January, 22, 1993. [7] Law No. 30 also revoked article 40 (on the criminalization of drug use) and article 41 (regulating the voluntary treatment of drug users) of Decree-Law No. 15/93.[8]

A. Use of Listed Substances

According to article 2(1) of Law No. 30/2000, the use, acquisition, and possession of plants, substances, or preparations listed in the abovementioned tables for a person's own consumption constitute misdemeanors (*contra-ordenaçãos*).[9] However, the acquisition and possession of these substances must not exceed the amount required for average personal use during a ten-day period.[10]

B. Jurisdiction for Processing and Execution

The processing of misdemeanors and the application of sanctions rest with the Commission for Drug Dissuasion (Comissão para a Dissuasão de Toxicodependência), which was specially created for this purpose and functions within dependent services facilities of the Institute for Drugs and Drug Addiction (Instituto da Droga e Toxicodependência) in each district.[11]

The administration of fines and alternative sanctions is the responsibility of the police.[12]

C. Apprehension and Identification

The police authorities must identify a user and eventually perform the search and seizure of plants, substances, or preparations referred to in article 1 of Law No. 30/2000 that are found in the possession of the user, which are forfeited to the state. The police must then prepare a report that is sent to the Commission with territorial jurisdiction.[13]

Where it is not possible to identify the user at the place and time of the occurrence, the police may, if necessary, detain the user to ensure his appearance before the Commission, subject to legal conditions governing detention for identification.[14]

D. Nature and Circumstances of Use

The Commission hears the drug user and gathers the other information (*elementos*) necessary to make a decision on whether the user is a drug addict, what substances were used, the circumstances and place of use, and the economic situation of the user. [15] The drug user can request the participation of a therapist, subject to regulation by the Commission.[16]

In making this decision, the Commission or the drug user may propose or request appropriate medical examinations, including but not limited to blood or urine tests.[17] If the Commission's determination was not based on such medical exams, the drug user may request them, and the results must be analyzed in a manner that enables the Commission to reassess its initial conclusion.[18]

The examination must be carried out by a properly authorized health service, or by a private service selected by the drug user, within thirty days.[19]

E. Treatment

If a drug user agrees to undergo treatment, the Commission communicates with the public or private health service chosen by the user, who must be informed of available alternatives.[20] The user is responsible for the costs of treatment provided by a private health service.[21]

The health service must inform the Commission every three months on whether to continue with the treatment.[22]

F. Provisional Suspension of Commission Proceedings

The Commission must provisionally suspend proceedings whenever a drug user without prior registration of misdemeanor proceedings under Law No. 30/2000 is considered a nonaddicted user,[23] whenever a drug user without registration of a prior misdemeanor proceeding under Law No. 30/2000 accepts to undergo treatment,[24] or if a drug user with a prior registration of misdemeanor proceedings under Law No. 30/2000 agrees to undergo treatment.[25] The decision to provisionally suspend proceedings is not appealable.[26]

G. Duration of Suspension

The proceedings may be suspended for up to two years and may be extended for another year by reasoned decision of the Commission.[27] The Commission must close and cannot reopen a case if a nonaddicted drug user has not relapsed or if an addicted user submits to treatment and does not improperly stop it.[28] The statute of limitations period does not run during the suspension of proceedings.[29]

H. Suspension of Sanction

The Commission may suspend the determination of the sanction if the drug user agrees to undergo voluntarily treatment.[30] The suspension period may last for up to three years.[31] If during the period of suspension the drug user stops treatment for reasons attributable to him or her, the suspension is revoked and the appropriate sanction for the underlying offense is determined.[32] The Commission declares the process closed if, after the suspension period, there is no reason that could lead to its revocation.[33]

I. Sanctions

1. Under Law No. 30

Nonaddicted drug users may be fined or, alternatively, subjected to a nonpecuniary sanction.[34] Nonpecuniary sanctions are also applicable to addicted users.[35] Pursuant to article 15(2), the Commission determines the penalty according to the need to prevent the use of narcotic drugs and psychotropic substances.[36] In the application of sanctions, the Commission takes into account the situation of the drug user and the nature and circumstances of drug use, considering, in particular,

a) the gravity of the act;
b) the agent's fault;
c) the type of plants, substances, or preparations consumed;
d) the public or private nature of consumption;
e) in the case of public consumption, the place of consumption;
f) in the event of a non-addicted user, the occasional or habitual nature of consumption;
g) the personal situation of the drug user, particularly his economic and financial situation.[37]

Instead of a fine, the Commission may impose a reprimand (*admoestação*) as an alternative.[38]

According to article 17(2) of Law No. 30/2000, without prejudice to the provision of article 15(2) of Law No. 30/2000, the Commission may impose the following sanctions as an alternative to a fine, or as the primary sanction:

a) prohibition on exercising a profession or activity, in particular those subject to a licensing regime, [that could] thereby result in risk to the safety of self or others;
b) prohibition on frequenting certain places;
c) prohibition on accompanying, lodging, or receiving certain persons;
d) prohibition on the absence of an alien without authorization;
e) periodic presentation in a place to be indicated by the commission;
f) suspension [or] prohibition on the concession and renewal of a license to use and carry a weapon of defense, hunting, or recreation;
g) seizure of items belonging to the drug user that pose a risk to the drug user or the community, or promote the commission of a crime or other offense; [or]
h) deprivation of grant management or a benefit awarded on a personal basis by public bodies or services, which will be entrusted to the entity that conducts the process or that accompanies the treatment process, when accepted.[39]

As an alternative to the abovementioned sanctions, the Commission may, provided that the drug user agrees, order him or her to provide compensation or public service to a public or private charitable institution, in accordance with the regime established in paragraphs 3 and 4 of article 58 of the Penal Code.[40] The Commission may suspend the execution of any of the mentioned sanctions, substituting them for the fulfillment of certain obligations under the terms of article 19 of Law No. 30/2000 (discussed below).

2. Under the Penal Code

Article 58(1) of the Penal Code determines that if a punishment not exceeding two years is to be applied, the court may replace it with a community service requirement if doing so is deemed an adequate and sufficient form of punishment.[41] The Penal Code defines "community service" as the provision of free services to the state, other public legal entities, or private organizations whose purposes the court considers of interest to the community.[42]

For the purposes of calculating the length of community service, each prison day established by the sentence is to be replaced by an hour of work, to a maximum of 480 hours.[43] Community service can be performed on Saturdays, Sundays, and holidays, as well as on weekdays, but may not affect normal working hours or exceed, per day, the overtime limits set by law.[44]

J. Fines

The range of potential fines differs depending on the table of Decree-Law No. 15 of January 22, 1993, the substances or preparations are listed on.[45]

Sixty percent of the proceeds of fines are distributed to the state and 40% to Intervention Service in Addictive Behaviors and Dependencies (Serviço de Intervenção nos Comportamentos Aditivos e nas Dependências, SICAD), formerly the Institute for Drugs and Drug Addiction.[46]

K. Reprimand

The Commission may simply give a reprimand if, taking into account the personal conditions of the drug user; the type of consumption; and the type of plants, substances, or preparations consumed, it believes that the user will refrain from use in the future.[47] A reprimand is an oral censorship, and the user must expressly be alerted to the consequences of his or her behavior and asked to refrain from further drug use.[48] The Commission must give the reprimand when the decision to apply the sanction is final,[49] and must deliver the reprimand immediately if the user renounces the right to appeal.[50]

L. Suspension of the Enforcement of the Sanction

In the case of an addicted drug user who refuses treatment or cannot be treated, the Commission may suspend enforcement of sanctions and require him or her to periodically appear before the health services. This suspension of the enforcement of sanctions may be subject to acceptance by the user of the measures provided for in article 19(3),[51] which provides that the Commission may propose other monitoring solutions advisable in specific cases.

In the case of a nonaddicted drug user, the Commission may opt for suspension of the sentence if, taking into account the personal conditions of the drug user; the type of consumption; and the type of plants, substances, or consumed preparations involved, it concludes that the purpose of preventing consumption is better served by this approach and the drug user accepts the conditions offered by the Commission under article 19(3) of Law No. 30/2000.[52]

Article 19(3) of Law No 30/2000 determines that the Commission may propose other monitoring solutions advisable for the circumstances of each case, in order to guarantee respect for the dignity of the individual and his or her acceptance of the measures set out in article 17(2)(a–d) of Law No. 30/2000.[53]

M. Duration of Suspended Enforcement of Sanctions

The suspension period for the enforcement of sanctions is set between one and three years after the final and nonappealable decision of the Commission, not counting the time the drug user is deprived of liberty by virtue of a coercive measure, criminal sentence, or security measure.[54] The Commission determines the duration of the measures provided for in article 19(3) of Law No. 30/2000, which cannot exceed the maximum limit of six months.[55]

N. Regular Presentation

Where enforcement of sanctions is suspended subject to the user's periodic appearance before the health services, the Commission makes the necessary communications to the health center of the user's home area or to another agreed upon health service.[56] The health center must inform the Commission on the regularity of appearances or noncompliance and the reasons for the noncompliance, if known.[57]

O. Communication of Measures

The decision to order the suspension of enforcement of sanctions must be communicated to those services and authorities whose cooperation with the enforcement measures was requested.[58] The services and authorities must communicate noncompliance to the Commission for the purposes of article 23(2) and (3) of Law No. 30/2000.[59]

P. Effects of the Suspension

The Commission declares the termination of the sanction if, after the suspension period, there is no reason that could lead to the revocation of the suspension decision.[60] Article 23(2) of Law No. 30/2000 determines that the suspension of a sanction is revoked whenever the drug user repeatedly breaches the imposed measures.[61] Article 23(3) establishes that the revocation of a suspension determines compliance with the applicable sanction.[62]

Q. Duration of the Sanctions

The sanctions provided for in article 17(2) of Law No. 30/2000 and the accompanying measures provided for in article 19 must have a minimum duration of one month and a maximum duration of three years.[63]

R. Fulfilment of the Sanctions and Accompanying Measures

The decision to impose sanctions or accompanying measures is reported to the police, and the police must inform the agencies (*serviços*) and authorities whose cooperation is needed for implementation of these measures.[64]

S. Subsidiary Law

In the absence of a specific provision of Law No. 30/2000, the general regime of administrative offenses must be applied.[65]

III. Decree-Law No. 130-A of April 23, 2001

According to the terms of Law No. 30/2000, the processing of the drug-related misdemeanors and the application of sanctions are the responsibility of the Commission for Drug Dissuasion.[66] On April 23, 2001, the government enacted Decree-Law No. 130-A to establish the organization, the process for the dissuasion of the drug user, and the Commission's operating system for the dissuasion of drug abuse and to regulate other supplementary matters.[67]

A. Territorial Jurisdiction

Offices of the Commission for Drug Dissuasion must be established in each district capital of the mainland within facilities made available by the Institute for Drugs and Drug Addiction (now, SICAD).[68] The Commission in the consumer's home area has territorial jurisdiction, unless the home area is not known, in which case the Commission in the area where the drug user was found has jurisdiction.[69]

B. Knowledge of the Offense

A police officer who becomes aware of an offense as provided for in Law No. 30/2000 must prepare a report describing

a) the facts that constitute the offense;
b) the date, time, place and circumstances in which the offense was committed;
c) all information available about the identification of the offender and his domicile;
d) the steps taken as well as the known evidence, including witnesses who can testify about the facts.[70]

The report is signed by the entity that prepared it and sent to the Commission with territorial jurisdiction by the fastest way possible, so that it is received by the Commission within thirty-six hours after the occurrence.[71] To prevent the disappearance of evidence, the police authorities confiscate the substances listed in the report and ship them within the shortest period of time to the Commission, to be deposited in the district's command.[72]

When it is not possible to identify the offender and the offender's place of residence at the time the offense occurs, the police may arrest the offender to enable his/her identification or to ensure his/her appearance before the Commission under the legal regime of detention for identification.[73] In this case, the offender may contact a family member or attorney by telephone.[74]

C. Preliminary Measures

When the offender reveals signs of physical or psychological decompensation, if the offender agrees or if the person's safety is in danger, the police authorities may take him or her to a public health service so that the necessary care can be provided; alternatively the police may, if possible, communicate to the Commission with territorial jurisdiction to allow it to adopt appropriate procedures.[75] Under these circumstances, the police must immediately send to the chairman of the Commission with territorial jurisdiction a report identifying the person, the date, and the reasons for the presentation.[76]

Once the report has been prepared, the drug user must be immediately notified by the police authority to appear before the Commission with territorial jurisdiction, which must occur in the shortest time possible, not to exceed seventy-two hours after the occurrence.[77]

When the offender discloses any disability, the police authorities must contact the person's legal representative in the shortest time possible in order to inform that person of the offense and provide notice to appear before the Commission.[78] The offender or his or her representative must be informed that they can hire an attorney, or require that an attorney be appointed.[79]

Decree-Law No. 130-A/2001 further details the composition (art. 3) and functions of the commission (arts. 4¥8); police procedures and hearings (arts. 12¥16); and several other procedures related to the processing of the offenses and the application of sanctions.

IV. Decree-Law No. 183 of June 21, 2001

Decree-Law No. 183 of June 21, 2001, approved the general system of prevention policies, which are aimed at the reduction of risk and the minimization of harm.[80]

A. Purpose

According to article 1, Decree-Law No. 183/2001 is intended to create programs and public health structures for the awareness and referral for treatment of drug addicts, prevent and reduce risky attitudes and behaviors, and minimize the individual and social harm caused by drug abuse.[81]

B. Duty of the State

For the protection of public health and the health of drug users, and in compliance with international obligations, the state bears the duty to make accessible to all drug users with risky attitudes and behaviors the abovementioned programs and structures, prioritized according to the specifics of each case.[82]

Whenever possible, partnerships with other public or private entities are encouraged.[83] To the extent possible, programs and structures must focus on referral for treatment and the cessation of drug use.[84]

For these purposes, the following programs and structures are regulated by this Decree-Law:

a) supporting offices for drug addicts;
b) reception centers;
c) shelter centers;
d) points of contact and information;

e) mobile spaces for the prevention of infectious diseases;
f) replacement programs;
g) needle-exchange programs;
h) street teams; [and]
i) programs for supervised use.[85]

1. Support Offices for Drug Addicts

The support offices for drug addicts (*gabinetes de apoio a toxicodependentes sem enquadramento sócio-familiar*) are places for screening, support, and referral for treatment.[86] The support offices are intended to contribute to the diagnosis and improvement of social and health conditions of marginalized and excluded drug users, and their referral for treatment.[87]

2. Reception Centers

Reception centers (*centros de acolhimento*) are temporary residential spaces. [88] They are designed to provide environments less conducive to drug use and to provide social and therapeutic treatment of excluded drug users.[89]

3. Shelter Centers

Shelter centers (*centros de abrigo*) are spaces for overnight stays.[90] The shelters aim to help improve sleeping conditions for drug users without social and family support, bring them closer to social systems, minimize the conditions that favor drug use, and provide for users' referral to treatment.[91]

4. Points of Contact and Information

Points of contact and information are spaces designed to prevent or reduce drug use and its risks.[92] These spaces are also used to educate the population about the risks and effects of drug addiction, and other issues that may contribute to the prevention of consumption.[93]

5. Mobile Spaces for the Prevention of Infectious Diseases

Mobile spaces for the prevention of infectious diseases are spaces for

a) the tracking and treatment of the most common infectious diseases in drug users;
b) the vaccination of the population at risk;

c) the reduction of injecting and/or smoking heroin on the street through the substitution of methadone, which must be dispensed in facilities assigned to projects in accordance with the law.[94]

6. Low-Demand Replacement Programs

Low-demand replacement programs (*programas de substituição em baixo limiar de exigência*) have the following objectives:

a) reduction in heroin use, by replacing it with methadone, to be dispensed through programs with great accessibility, without requiring immediate abstinence and in adequate facilities for this purpose;
b) increase in the regularity of contacts of drug users with professionals from a public health team that can particularly help with the person's future abstinence.[95]

7. Needle Exchange Programs

The purpose of needle exchange programs is to prevent the transmission of infectious diseases intravenously.[96] The programs are designed to promote accessibility to the exchange of syringes and needles, filters, wipes, distilled water, citric acid, and other suitable materials.[97]

8. Street Teams

Street teams (*equipas de rua*) are designed to promote the reduction of risks, by intervening in public spaces where drug use is experienced as a social problem.[98]

9. Programs for Supervised Use

The objective of the programs for supervised use (*programas para consumo vigiado*) are to increase infection-free intravenous use and the consequent reduction of risks associated with this form of use, and to get closer to drug users in their socio-cultural context, with a view to building their awareness and referring them to treatment, through the creation of sites for this type of use.[99]

COUNTRIES THAT ALLOW TREATMENT AND ALTERNATIVE PUNISHMENTS FOR MINOR OFFENSES

ARGENTINA

Graciela Rodriguez-Ferrand
Senior Foreign Law Specialist

Argentina's Law 23737 of 1989 punishes drug possession with imprisonment of one to six years and a fine.[1] Article 14 of the Law also punishes the possession of small quantities of drugs for personal use. However, the penalty in such cases is imprisonment for one month to two years, which can be replaced by detoxification and rehabilitation treatment.[2]

In the 2009 *Arriola* decision[3] the Supreme Court declared the penalty provision (second paragraph) of article 14 unconstitutional as a violation of article 19 of the National Constitution (NC), which provides as follows:

> The private actions of individuals, which in no way offend public order or morality, nor injure a third party, are only reserved to God and are exempted from the authority of judges. No inhabitant of the Nation shall be obliged to perform what the law does not demand nor deprived of what it does not prohibit.[4]

The *Arriola* case involved five individuals who were arrested when leaving their house with small quantities of marijuana. The Supreme Court concluded that criminalizing the possession of drugs for personal use when it does not pose any danger or harm to others is a violation of NC article 19.[5] It also ruled that personal use protected under the NC must not affect others, and that possession for personal use must be determined by the small quantity of the drug in question.

The ruling does not specifically state what amounts are considered "small amounts" for personal-use purposes. The broad language used in the ruling, coupled with the fact that decisions rendered by the Supreme Court are only applicable to each individual case and do not bind other lower courts, has led other courts to continue prosecuting drug users.[6] Therefore, each judge has the authority to determine the quantity and circumstances that qualify as "personal use."[7]

In the *Arriola* case, the Supreme Court did not decriminalize the use of marijuana in general. It only ruled that it is unconstitutional to impose criminal penalties on an adult who consumes a small amount of marijuana in a private setting with no harm to others.[8]

On April 2016, the government reportedly announced that it will send a bill to Congress that would amend Law 23737 to set clear limits and amounts on drugs for purposes of establishing personal use in order to avoid the confusion created by the *Arriola* decision.[9]

AUSTRALIA

Kelly Buchanan

Chief, Foreign, Comparative, and International Law Division I

Summary

Australian state and territory legislation contains offenses related to illicit drugs. Cannabis and other illicit substances are illegal throughout the country. In three jurisdictions, however, certain minor offenses, primarily involving possession of small amounts of cannabis or smoking implements, may be dealt with by way of an infringement notice, with a fine to be paid within a specified period in order for the person to avoid being charged with an offense. In addition, in line with initiatives developed under the National Drug Strategy, all states and territories operate "diversion" programs aimed at diverting people apprehended for certain minor drug offenses from the criminal justice system and into education or treatment programs. Diversion programs are operated by the police, who may caution and refer individuals to education or intervention sessions, as well as by the courts. In some jurisdictions, specialized drug courts have the ability to refer offenders to treatment and rehabilitation services and to monitor their progress.

I. Introduction

The Commonwealth of Australia is a federation of six states, two mainland self-governing territories, and several external territories. Each state and self-governing territory has laws prohibiting the cultivation, manufacture, sale or supply, possession, and use of specified drugs. Federal criminal laws also contain drug offenses, including offenses related to importing and exporting narcotics.[1]

A National Drug Strategy, involving some nongovernment organizations as well as all Australian governments, has been in place since 1985. The aims of the strategy are "improving health, social and economic outcomes for Australians by preventing the uptake of harmful drug use and reducing the harmful effects of licit and illicit drugs in our society."[2] Consultation on a new strategy covering the years 2016–2025 is currently being undertaken. The draft strategy

> describes a nationally agreed harm minimisation approach to reducing the harm arising from alcohol, tobacco and other drug use. As well as outlining the national commitment to the harm minimisation approach, the strategy describes priority actions, groups and drug types and summarises effective demand, supply and harm reduction strategies. The strategy also includes headline indicators to monitor success.[3]

While there is no national decriminalization policy, and recreational cannabis cultivation, sale, possession, and use is illegal across the country, three jurisdictions (Australian Capital Territory, South Australia, and Northern Territory) have decriminalized minor cannabis offenses. Other states have introduced drug diversion programs where offenders are cautioned and may be referred to an education or intervention program rather than being charged with minor drug offenses. According to the Australian Institute of Criminology,

> [i]n line with the National Illicit Drug Strategy, Australian states and territories have introduced initiatives to divert some drug users away from courts and the criminal justice system. There are two main streams of diversion: directly to treatment or education programs or the issuing of an infringement or on the spot fine. Infringement systems are legislatively based, while some treatment diversion systems rely on restricting the discretion of police to arrest, rather than legislation.[4]

The Australian Institute of Health and Welfare states that

> [p]olice and court drug diversion programs expanded markedly in Australia from 1999 when the Australian, state and territory governments established the Illicit Drug Diversion Initiative (IDDI). Supported by Australian Government funding and a national framework, the IDDI enabled new and/or expanded drug diversion programs to be set in place in all states and territories and led to the 'development of a more systematic approach to diversion.'[5]

Separate from the National Drug Strategy and related initiatives, the federal Parliament enacted legislation in February 2016 that provides for the legalization and regulation of medicinal cannabis products.[6] It includes a national licensing system for the controlled cultivation of cannabis for medicinal or scientific purposes. In effect, the legislation will mean that "a patient with a valid prescription can possess and use a medicinal cannabis product manufactured from cannabis plants legally cultivated in Australia, where the supply is appropriately authorized under the Therapeutic Goods Act 1989 and relevant state and territory legislation."[7] To date, Victoria,[8] New South Wales,[9] and Tasmania[10] have taken action to provide people in those states with the ability to access medicinal cannabis products that have been produced in accordance with the federal law. The Queensland government has also introduced a bill on the subject.[11]

II. State-Level Decriminalization of Minor Drug Offenses

As noted above, three Australian jurisdictions have decriminalized certain minor drug offenses, particularly related to cannabis possession, while others have diversion programs that allow people to avoid conviction for such offenses if they attend specific programs.[12] The relevant legislation and policies of each state and territory are outlined below.

A. Australian Capital Territory

Under the Simple Cannabis Offence Notice (SCON) system of the Australian Capital Territory a person may "possess up to 50 grams of dried cannabis, OR one or two cannabis plants (excluding all hydroponically or artificially cultivated cannabis plants) for personal use only."[13] A fine of AU$100 (about US$75) applies to such offenses, which are called "simple cannabis offences." It is possible to pay the fine online.[14] If the fine is paid within sixty days, "no criminal record will be recorded."[15] As possession of any amount of cannabis remains illegal, police have the discretion to issue a SCON or charge an offender with a criminal offense.[16]

The SCON system was introduced in 1992.[17] Originally, the amendments to the Drugs of Dependence Act 1989 (ACT) allowed up to five cannabis plants to be dealt with by way of a SCON,[18] but this was reduced to "one or two" by amending legislation passed in 2004, which also excluded artificial or hydroponic cultivation from the simple offense.[19] In 2013, the Act was amended to increase the allowable amount of cannabis that may be subject to a SCON from twenty-five grams to fifty grams.[20]

In 2014, the *Canberra Times* reported that around five hundred notices had been issued for simple cannabis offenses in the preceding five years.[21] A spokeswoman for ACT Policing said that the notice system streamlined police procedures and reduced court time, and that "[a]dditional benefits beyond the avoidance of a court experience and possible criminal conviction for the offender are perceived to be a reduction in the contact between the average user and the criminal element involved in dealing drugs."[22] Furthermore, she said that the system reduced the time and resources police spend on minor offenses, allowing them to focus on the cannabis black market. According to the news report, those issued with a notice can choose to attend a drug assessment and treatment program rather than paying the fine.[23]

The ACT also operates Diversion Service programs "aimed at diverting people arrested and/or charged with drug or alcohol related offences out of the judicial system into the health system."[24] This includes Police Early Diversion, where police officers refer persons apprehended for possession of small amounts of illicit drugs to the Alcohol and Drug Program Diversion Service for assessment and subsequent treatment referrals.[25]

B. New South Wales

While New South Wales has not decriminalized cannabis possession, which is an offense under the Drug Misuse and Trafficking Act 1985 (NSW),[26] police in the state have "official discretion to caution adults for minor cannabis offences, and to caution people under 18 for minor offences involving any prohibited drug." [27] The Cannabis Cautioning Scheme has been in place since 2000.[28]

Under the official police guidelines for the Cannabis Cautioning Scheme, if an adult is found in possession of less than fifteen grams of cannabis, or using cannabis, or in possession of smoking implements, police officers can use their discretion to issue an official caution, rather than charging the person with an offense. Such cautions are issued on the spot and the person will be provided with information about the legal status of cannabis and the harms associated with cannabis. The person's name and address is also recorded in the police computer system. If the person receives a second caution, he or she is "referred to a compulsory drug education session."[29]

In order to qualify for a caution, the person must

- admit the offence
- have no criminal history for drug offences (including possession), sexual assault or other offences involving violence
- have received no more than two cannabis cautions previously
- establish their identity (normal checks on identity will be carried out)
- satisfy the police that the cannabis is for personal use only
- have no other charges that must be determined in court anyway. (For example, if the police find a few grams of cannabis in the pocket of a person charged with stealing, both the theft charge and the drug possession charge will go to court.)[30]

People under the age of eighteen may be issued a caution for minor offenses involving cannabis and other drugs, including cannabis cultivation. The cautioning system "is part of a range of alternative systems under the Young Offenders Act 1997 (NSW) to divert young people from courts and prisons."[31] Under this legislation, the following drug offenses can be dealt with by way of a police caution:

- possession of 15 grams of cannabis or less
- possession of smoking implements
- cultivation of no more than five cannabis plants
- possession of no more than one gram of heroin, cocaine or amphetamine
- possession of no more than 0.0008 grams of LSD
- possession of no more than 0.25 grams of ecstasy
- use of a prohibited drug.[32]

To be eligible for a caution, the young person must admit the offense and there must be no other offenses that would require the person to go to court. Police must accept that the drugs are for personal use rather than supply.

Different from the adult caution system, juvenile cautions are issued by a police officer or other official about a week after the offense, rather than on the spot. There are no limits on the number of cautions that can be issued, although police always have the discretion to bring charges.[33]

The Drug Court of New South Wales was the first to be trialed and evaluated in Australia. The Court has sentencing discretion to require an offender to participate in an ongoing rehabilitation program under court supervision. If the offender agrees to the program, any penalty imposed by the Court is suspended and the person's completion of the program is taken into account in determining the final sentence.[34]

C. Northern Territory

Under the Misuse of Drugs Act (NT), police in the Northern Territory have discretion to issue infringement notices to adults found in possession of up to fifty grams of cannabis plant material, one gram of cannabis oil, ten grams of cannabis resin or cannabis seed, or two non-hydroponic plants.[35] A person served with an infringement or "on the spot" notice is subject to a fine of AU$200 (about US$150) and has twenty-eight days to pay the fine in order to avoid a criminal charge.[36] Infringement notices were introduced through legislation enacted in 1996.

Persons under the age of seventeen may not receive infringement notices and will instead be prosecuted in court.[37]

The Northern Territory also participates in the national Illicit Drug Diversion Initiative through two main programs: the NT Illicit Drug Pre Court Diversion Program (NTIDPCDP), which is overseen by the Department of Health and NT Police, and the Court Referral and Evaluation for Drug Intervention and Treatment Program (CREDIT NT), which is overseen by the Department of Justice and operated by the Magistrates Court.[38] The NTIDPCDP commenced in 2002 and is "available to first time offenders for use and possession of any illicit substance."[39] CREDIT NT is "a bail program which provides support for defendants with substance abuse problems by providing access to drug treatment and rehabilitation, accommodation and other supports."[40]

D. Queensland

The Queensland police service operates a drug diversion program where people arrested or questioned for a minor drug offense have an "opportunity to receive professional help to quit using drugs, rather than going through the normal court process and getting a criminal record."[41] The diversion program was established by legislation enacted in 2000.[42] The Queensland Police website states that

> [m]ost drug offences in Queensland involve possession of small amounts of cannabis. A court appearance without appropriate health interventions has not been successful in reducing cannabis use or drug related offences. The PDDP [Police Drug Diversion Program] offers people apprehended for a minor drugs offence with an opportunity to receive professional help through early intervention and prevention, to address their drug use, before proceeding through the normal court process and incurring a criminal record.[43]

The program is available for people caught with up to fifty grams of cannabis or in possession of a smoking implement.[44] Only one offer of diversion is permitted. The person must not have committed another indictable offense related to the drug offense and must not have been previously sentenced to a term of imprisonment under certain provisions of the Drugs Misuse Act 1986 (Qld)[45] or convicted of an offense involving violence. The person must also admit having committing the minor drug offense. A child who has been previously cautioned for a minor drug offense must be offered the diversion program.[46]

The person is given and asked to sign a form titled "Minor Drugs Offence Diversion (Agreement to Attend and Requirement to Comply)," requiring him or her to attend and complete a Drug Diversion Assessment Programme (DDAP) with an approved Queensland Health service provider.[47] The DDAP session, which takes about two hours, includes an assessment of the person's drug use, involving questions about how often he or she uses drugs and any problems that may influence that usage, and education on the "health effects of illicit drug use and the legal consequences of continued use."[48] The provider will then work with the person to develop a plan to help stop him or her using illicit drugs. This might include the provision of information about, and referral to, a voluntary treatment program for drug dependence. The person is encouraged to take a friend or family member to the session.[49]

"Court diversion" is also available for persons who appear before the Magistrate's Court or Children's Court on charges involving certain minor drug possession offenses.[50] People under seventeen years of age will be given the chance to attend a drug education and information session in order to avoid conviction, while adults will be asked to sign a document in which he or she agrees to be of good behavior for a period of time and to attend a drug education and information session.[51] Examples of minor offenses for which an adult may qualify for court diversion include fifty grams of cannabis, one gram of heroin, one gram of methadone, one gram of amphetamine, one gram of cocaine, and three tickets or tabs of LSD. The full list of what is considered minor amounts for different drugs is provided by regulations.[52]

E. South Australia

Under South Australia's Controlled Substances Act 1984 (SA), minor offenses involving personal possession of small amounts of cannabis, cannabis resin, or smoking equipment may be dealt with by way of an on the spot fine.[53] Such fines, or "expiation fees," are applied to "simple cannabis offences" by way of an expiation notice given under the Expiation of Offences Act 1996 (SA).[54] The limits under the Act are one hundred grams of marijuana, twenty grams of resin, one non-hydroponic plant, or cannabis smoking equipment,[55] and the fines range from between AU$150 (about US$112) and AU$300 (about US$224) depending on the offense,[56] with a person having sixty days to pay in order to avoid being charged with an offense.[57]

The infringement notice and fine system first came into effect in 1987,[58] making South Australia the first Australian jurisdiction to decriminalize possession of minor amounts of cannabis.

South Australia Police also operate the Police Drug Diversion Initiative, with Drug and Alcohol Services SA responsible for statewide coordination of the program and supporting health workers in administering the program.[59] Under the Controlled Substances Act 1984 (SA), a police officer must refer a person who is alleged to have committed a simple drug possession offense to a nominated assessment service.[60] For adults, this applies to all illicit substances other than cannabis (to which an expiation notice applies) and for children aged ten to seventeen years it applies to all drugs.[61]

F. Tasmania

According to a 2014 Tasmanian government report,

> [t]he Tasmanian Illicit Drug Diversion Initiative (IDDI) program (Police Diversion) is a discretionary police diversion program aimed at eligible drug offenders who are at the early stages of contact with the criminal justice system. The Tasmanian component of the Police diversion program provides for the diversion of offenders apprehended by Tasmania Police officers for the use of small quantities of illicit drugs (mainly cannabis) to drug treatment services. The Tasmanian framework uses existing police discretion and 'Commissioners Instructions' to allow Tasmania Police officers to divert

> eligible offenders to education, assessment and treatment. The level of diversion is proportional to the nature of the offence.[62]

The youth justice legislation and police policy also allow police to issue informal and formal cautions to young people in relation to drug possession and use. If a formal caution is issued, "attendance at a health diversion can be mandated."[63]

In addition, the Magistrates Court of Tasmania operates a Court Mandated Diversion program that allows magistrates to divert eligible offenders into drug treatment. The program commenced as pilot in 2007. Under the program, "[f]ollowing a plea or finding of guilt, eligible and suitable individuals can be diverted into drug treatment through sentencing to a Drug Treatment Order (DTO) where a Magistrate will continually review the individual's progress on the order. A DTO is an intensive community based sentence that has a custodial sentence attached."[64] To be eligible for a DTO a person must be over eighteen years of age, have entered guilty pleas or been found guilty of the relevant offenses, be facing a penalty of imprisonment, have a demonstrable history of illicit drug use that contributed to the offense(s), and be willing to participate in supervised treatment.[65]

G. Victoria

Victoria has not decriminalized cannabis. However, police in Victoria are able to issue a caution (Cannabis Caution) to individuals over the age of seventeen who are caught with a small quantity of cannabis (less than fifty grams), provided it is the person's first or second offense and he or she admits to the possession.[66] A police officer may refer a person to attend an education session to learn about the effects of cannabis and how to stop taking the drug.[67] The Cannabis Caution program was initiated in 1997.[68] A caution is available for possession and use offenses under the Drugs, Poisons and Controlled Substances Act 1981 (Vic).[69]

People caught with small amounts of other drugs, and who admit to having the drugs, may also be given Drug Diversion by the police. This program, which was first piloted in 1998,[70] requires the offender to attend two appointments at a drug treatment agency in order to avoid a criminal record. To be eligible for the Drug Diversion program a person must be over ten years of age, have been arrested for a small amount of illicit drugs other than cannabis, admit the offense, and not have any more than one previous cautioning notice (including a Cannabis Caution).[71] People are not eligible for either a Cannabis Caution or for diversion if they are trafficking, are involved in other offenses at the time, have a prescription drug without a prescription, or do not admit the offense.[72]

Drug offenses are tried in a separate court, the Drug Court, which has different sentencing options. This includes the availability of suspended prison sentences for two years while a person undertakes a Drug Treatment Order. Persons subject to such an order must undergo regular testing, attend drug and alcohol counseling, see a case manager and clinical adviser, and come before a Drug Court Magistrate on a regular basis. [73] Other programs include the Children's Court Clinic Drug Program, which "provides early intervention drug treatment for young people appearing in the criminal division of the court who have demonstrated substance misuse."[74]

H. Western Australia

Western Australia introduced civil penalties for certain minor cannabis offenses in 2003 (effective from 2004),[75] but this law was overturned in 2010 (effective from 2011).[76]

Since 2011, Western Australia Police have operated a Cannabis Intervention Requirement (CIR) program under which offenders aged fourteen years or over who are caught with less than ten grams of cannabis and/or a smoking implement with traces of cannabis can be given a CIR. The CIR can be resolved by the person attending a Cannabis Intervention Session within twenty-eight days. These one-hour sessions are run by approved drug counselors and aim to increase awareness about the laws and health effects associated with cannabis use, as well as encouraging discussion and changes in behavior. If the person does not attend a session, the alleged offense will be prosecuted.[77]

An adult can receive only one CIR while a younger person aged fourteen to seventeen years can be given two CIRs.[78] A young person who commits a third minor cannabis offense will, where appropriate, be referred to a Juvenile Justice Team, rather than being charged.[79] The program does not apply to offenses involving possession or cultivation of cannabis plants, or possession of cannabis resin, cannabis oil, or other cannabis derivatives.[80]

The CIR program is legislated under the Misuse of Drugs Act 1981 (WA)[81] and the Young Offenders Act 1994 (WA).[82]

A further program, which is also part of the WA Diversion Program, is the Other Drug Intervention Requirement. This initiative "provides assessment and treatment for adults and juveniles for simple possession of illicit drugs.

There is emphasis on positive action (not necessarily prosecution) including diversion from the judicial system and referral to treatment services."[83] A person issued an Other Drug Intervention Requirement notice must attend three intervention sessions within forty-two days; if necessary, ongoing support may be made available. The program is primarily for adults who have no previous drug convictions, and a notice can only be issued once.[84]

In addition, Western Australia has both an adult and children's drug court,[85] and "[c]ourt diversion programs are available to most offenders appearing in court who have drug-related problems, depending on the seriousness of the offence."[86]

BRAZIL

Eduardo Soares
Senior Foreign Law Specialist

I. Introduction

Brazil has not decriminalized narcotics. However, with the promulgation of Law No. 11,343 on August 23, 2006,[1] Brazil changed its approach to the penalization of those caught with drugs for alleged personal use. Although still a crime, instead of imposing prison time as a form of punishment, the law opted for alternative punishments.

II. Law No. 11,343 of August 23, 2006

According to article 28 of Law No. 11,343, whoever acquires, keeps, stores, transports, or carries for personal use drugs without authorization or in violation of a legal or regulatory determination, is subject to the following punishments:

I – receive a warning about the effects of drugs;
II – render community services; [or]
III – . . . attend a program or educational course.[2]

The same punishment applies to those who, for their own use, plant, cultivate, or harvest crops for the preparation of a small amount of substance or product capable of causing physical or psychological dependence.[3] To determine whether the drug was intended for personal use, the judge must consider the nature and quantity of the substance seized, the place and the conditions under which the actions developed, social and personal circumstances, and the person's conduct and prior behavior.[4]

The law continues to criminalize and punish with five to fifteen years in prison and a fine those persons who import, export, ship, prepare, produce, manufacture, purchase, sell, display for sale, offer, store, transport, bring, keep, prescribe, administer, deliver, or provide drugs for use, although free, without authorization or in violation of legal or regulatory requirements.[5]

III. Extraordinary Appeal

On February 22, 2011, an extraordinary appeal (*recurso extraordinário*)[6] was filed with the Brazilian Federal Supreme Court (Supremo Tribunal Federal, STF) questioning the compatibility of article 28 of Law 11,343, which criminalizes the possession of drugs for personal use, with the constitutional principles of intimacy and privacy.[7] The case is still pending before the STF.

IV. Proposed Legislation

A bill was introduced in the Chamber of Deputies on July 14, 2010, to add and amend provisions of Law No. 11,343, of August 23, 2006. The purpose of the bill is to discuss the National Drug Policy System (Sistema Nacional de Políticas sobre Drogas), to provide for the mandatory classification of drugs, to introduce aggravating circumstances to the crimes set forth in articles 33 through 37, to define the conditions of attention to drug users or drug addicts, and to deal with the funding of policies on drugs.[8] On May 28, 2013, after the bill was discussed and voted on, it was forwarded to the Federal Senate where it is currently under consideration.[9]

GERMANY

Jenny Gesley
Foreign Law Specialist

Summary

In general, dealing in narcotics in Germany without a license or a prescription from a doctor is illegal and subject to punishment according to sections 29 to 30a of the Narcotic Drugs Act. The Narcotic Drugs Act authorizes the German states to establish drug consumption rooms in which drug-addicted persons are allowed to use narcotic drugs that they bring with them and that have not been medically prescribed. Furthermore, the prosecutors' offices and the courts have discretion to refrain from prosecution or punishment if the suspect possessed or procured small quantities of narcotics for personal use only.

I. General Overview

Narcotic drugs encompass all substances and preparations listed in annexes I to III of the German Narcotic Drugs Act.[1] The narcotics are divided into non-trafficable substances (Annex I), trafficable substances that are not prescribable (Annex II), and trafficable and prescribable substances (Annex III). There is no distinction between soft and hard drugs in order to emphasize that the provisions of the Narcotic Drugs Act apply equally to all narcotics and that the different risks and hazards of substances and preparations will only be taken into account at sentencing.[2]

Section 2 of the Narcotic Drugs Act defines substances and preparations. Substances are "chemical elements and chemical compounds, as well as their naturally occurring mixtures and solutions; plants, algae, fungi and lichens, as well as their parts and components in a processed or unprocessed state; bodies of animals, also live animals, as well as human and animal body parts, components and metabolites in a processed or unprocessed state; [and] microorganisms including viruses, as well as their components or metabolites." Preparations are defined as "mixtures of substances or the solutions of one or several substances except the natural mixtures and solutions."

In general, dealing in narcotics requires a license from the Federal Institute for Drugs and Medical Devices.[3] For substances listed in Annex I, a license can only be granted for scientific or other purposes in the public interest.[4] Cannabis is listed as a plant in Annex I. Dealing in narcotics without a license or a prescription from a doctor is generally illegal and subject to punishment according to sections 29 to 30a of the Narcotic Drugs Act. Dealing includes cultivating, producing, trading, importing, exporting, distributing, selling, otherwise placing narcotics on the market, acquiring, or producing exempt preparations of narcotics.[5]

Exceptions from the obligation to obtain a license exist for pharmacies; veterinary practice dispensaries; anyone who acquires narcotic drugs listed in Annex III on the basis of a prescription; anyone who exports or imports narcotic drugs listed in Annex III as a physician, dentist, or veterinarian as part of cross-border services or as travel necessities; anyone who on a commercial basis is involved in the transport of narcotic drugs between authorized participants in the trade in narcotic drugs; or anyone who acquires narcotic drugs listed in Annex I, II, or III as a subject or patient in the context of a clinical trial or in hardship cases.[6] Further exceptions are listed in the annexes for certain substances.

II. Drug Consumption Rooms

In 2000, the German legislature enacted a provision that authorized the German state governments to establish drug consumption rooms.[7] Drug consumption rooms are facilities in which drug-addicted persons are allowed to use narcotic drugs that they bring with them and that have not been medically prescribed.[8] Drug consumption rooms are supposed to further the goal of harm reduction, which had become part of the international and German drug policy in the preceding years. Thus far, only Berlin, Hamburg, Hesse, Lower Saxony, North Rhine-Westphalia, and Saarland have enacted such regulations.[9] The regulations must set minimum standards to ensure security and control of the use of narcotics in drug consumption rooms.[10] The law provides that the prosecutor cannot prosecute people who use drugs in drug consumption rooms.[11]

III. Possession of Small Quantities for Personal Use

Prosecutors and courts have discretion to refrain from prosecution or punishment if the suspect cultivates, produces, imports, exports, carries in transit, acquires, otherwise procures, or possesses narcotic drugs merely in small quantities for his or her personal use.[12] The Act does not define what constitutes a small quantity. Instead, what constitutes a small quantity varies for the different types of narcotics and has been determined by the courts. The Federal Court of Justice held that in order to determine the threshold amount for a small quantity, the quantity of the active ingredient and not the weight is relevant. A small quantity of cannabis, for example, is a substance that contains 7.5 grams of THC or less.[13]

In 1994, the Federal Constitutional Court criticized the fact that the prosecutors' offices in the German states all had different approaches for the prosecution of the possession of small quantities of narcotics for personal use and demanded uniform implementation of the law.[14] The Court suggested that the states should issue guidelines for prosecutors, which all states except for Bremen, Mecklenburg-West Pomerania, and Thuringia have done.[15]

ISRAEL

Ruth Levush

Senior Foreign Law Specialist

Summary

Israeli law generally criminalizes the possession and use of narcotics listed as "dangerous drugs," including cannabis. Although the law imposes severe penalties on offenders, as a matter of policy the prosecution is instructed to close criminal files involving offenders the law refers to as "normative persons." Such files are to be closed with a warning and under specific requirements if such offenders do not have criminal records and were caught for the first time with a small amount of marijuana or hashish for personal consumption.

The Israel Anti-Drug Authority objects to legalization of all drugs and does not distinguish between "light" and "heavy" drugs. Several private member bills, however, have been introduced by Knesset

Members in recent years with regard to offenses involving cannabis. These bills either call for reduction of penalties for certain offenders possessing or consuming cannabis for personal consumption, or call for decriminalization of certain types of cannabis products or strains, such as those containing natural cannabidiol (CBD) or tetrahydrocannabinol (THC) lower than 0.2%, or those considered medical cannabis. These bills are at the preliminary stage and have not been forwarded for further legislative consideration at this time.

I. Criminalization of Possession and Use of Dangerous Drugs

The possession and use of "dangerous drugs" in Israel are generally prohibited. Possession is permitted, however, for authorized pharmacists, physicians, veterinarians, and persons who received the drugs from authorized medical professionals. [1] The use of dangerous drugs is similarly permitted if used for medical reasons when the drugs were dispensed by authorized medical professionals.[2]

The Law defines "dangerous drugs" as any of the substances that are listed in its first schedule. The list currently includes, among others, "any type of the plant of cannabis and every part of it, including its roots, but excluding the oil that derives from its seeds."[3]

The unauthorized possession or use of dangerous drugs constitutes a criminal offense punishable by twenty years' imprisonment or a fine at a rate of 5,650,000 Israel Shekels (ILS) (about US$1,468,646). Where possession or use is for personal consumption the penalty is reduced to three years' imprisonment or a fine of 226,000 ILS (about US$58,789).[4] However, a minor under the age of sixteen convicted of possessing or using dangerous drugs on the premises of a school where he or she is not a student is subject to five years' imprisonment.[5]

II. Implementation Policy

Notwithstanding the Law's penalty structure, a directive issued by Israel's Attorney General states that cases involving use or possession of dangerous drugs by "normative persons" who do not otherwise have a criminal record, and who were caught for the first time possessing or using a small amount of marijuana or hashish for personal consumption, should not generally be subject to full enforcement of the Law.[6] Files closed under these circumstances should be labeled as closed for lack of public interest in full implementation, considering the suspect's first-time drug offense perpetrated for personal consumption.[7]

To be authorized for closure the following conditions should be met:

- The suspect has confessed;
- The suspect has filed a request to close the file; has committed to not using any more dangerous drugs in the future; and declared that he/she is aware that if caught again he/she would be subject to the full force of the law also for the first offense, subject to the statute of limitations;
- There are no other criminal records of the suspect's involvement in drugs, property, or violent offenses, or "other relevant offenses;" and
- There are no aggravating circumstances, such as when the suspect was responsible for the safety of others.[8]

III. Anti-Drug Authority's Position on Decriminalization of Narcotics

The Israel Anti-Drug Authority (IADA) is a statutory corporation established by the National Authority for Fighting Drugs and Misuse of Alcohol Law, 5748-1988. [9] According to its website, "IADA is a quasi-governmental agency, which operates under the aegis of the Prime Minister. In 2009, the Israel Knesset approved a decision granting the Ministry of Public Security responsibility for IADA."[10]

The IADA objects to legalization of all drugs and does not distinguish between "light" and "heavy" drugs. It specifically rejects the claim made by "a small, vocal, and noisy minority, which tries to convince youth that the use of cannabis products causes limited damage or no harm at all especially regarding marijuana."[11] According to the IADA there are approximately two hundred types of marijuana currently available. The main difference among them, it states, is in the concentration of their active ingredient, tetrahydrocannabinol (THC). As compared with the 1960s, when the percentage of THC did not exceed 4%, there are currently types of marijuana with a 25% concentration of THC, the IADA's website states. Consumption of THC, according to the IADA, disrupts brain activity and has a negative impact on memory, coordination, and the ability to concentrate.[12]

The IADA does recognize that in certain circumstances criminal prosecution may be replaced by other approaches. These include sending suspects caught for the first time to drug rehabilitation and treatment in lieu of being processed in the criminal justice system, and imposing lenient or delayed sentences on such offenders. The IADA also supports the distribution of clean syringes to addicts, to prevent the spread of AIDS and other contagious diseases.

IV. Bills for Decriminalization or Penalty Reduction for Cannabis Offenses

Several private member bills have been proposed by Knesset Members (KMs) in recent years addressing offenses involving cannabis.[13] These bills can generally be divided into two types: bills that call for the reduction of penalties for certain offenders possessing or consuming cannabis for personal consumption, and bills that call for the decriminalization of certain types of cannabis products. The following is a brief summary of some recent draft bills from both groups.

A. Reduction of Penalties for Certain Offenders

The latest draft bill was introduced on May 23, 2016, by KMs Sharren Haskel[14] and Dov Henin.[15] The bill calls for a significant reduction in the severe penalties for adults over twenty-one years of age if, at the time of committing an offense involving possession or use of cannabis, they did not commit additional offenses punishable by three months' imprisonment or a fine.

The bill proposes to subject such offenders to a fine of up to 300 ILS (about US$78), or up to 1,500 ILS if the offense was committed in a public place.[16]

Explanatory notes to the bill state that it was not designed to encourage cannabis use. Instead, it is designed "to prevent transforming normative adults over 21 into criminals in the eyes of the law."[17] According to the explanatory notes, the bill would save "huge amounts invested in law enforcement" and relieve the burden on the justice system, "which is required to handle thousands of criminal files for use and possession of cannabis for personal use every year."[18]

B. Decriminalization of Certain Types of Cannabis Strains or Products

A draft bill submitted by KMs Sharren Haskel on March 30, 2016, calls for excluding cannabidiol (CBD) from the cannabis products the possession or consumption of which are criminal offenses. [19] Noting the numerous, known medical advantages of CBD, the bill's explanatory notes provide that many American and European companies have been investing in the development of synthetic CBD. Unlike natural CBD, synthetic CBD causes side effects for users. According to the explanatory notes, a unique strain of natural CBD has been developed and exists only in Israel. Calling for decriminalization of CBD, the explanatory notes state that natural CBD does not require patent registration, has many medical advantages, does not cause the feeling of floating otherwise caused by synthetic CBD, and represents the potential for significant income to the state.[20]

Another draft bill introduced on March 28, 2016, calls for excluding medical cannabis from cannabis products that are considered dangerous drugs under the Law. Currently, the distribution of cannabis for medical purposes requires special authorization by the Medical Cannabis Unit in the Ministry of Health.[21] The bill proposes facilitating the dispersion of medical cannabis by medical professionals and pharmacists, or other authorized persons.[22] The draft bill defines "medical cannabis" as cannabis that underwent the necessary procedures for adjustment for medical use—either in the form of powder, oil, food, or in another way— including all the endocannabinoids that exist in it in a natural way.[23]

A draft bill introduced by six Knesset Members on February 29, 2016, proposes to exclude industrial strains of cannabis from cannabis that is considered a dangerous drug. The draft bill defines "industrial strain of cannabis" as one with a THC level lower than 0.2% and which was approved by the Minister of Agriculture and Rural Development or recognized as an industrial strain by the European Union.[24] Similar draft bills legalizing the use of industrial stains of cannabis were submitted in the preceding session of the Knesset.[25]

NEW ZEALAND

Kelly Buchanan
Chief, Foreign, Comparative, and International Law Division I

Summary

New Zealand has not decriminalized possession or use of cannabis or other drugs, but has diversion programs that allow the police or prosecutors to divert minor offenders from the criminal justice system and into treatment or counseling. In addition, a drug court, the Alcohol and Other Drug Treatment Court, is currently operating in one major city under a five-year pilot program that commenced in 2012.

Where there has been a major shift in approach is in relation to new psychoactive substances, such as "party pills" and synthetic cannabis. Such substances were previously legal unless they had been criminalized under the Misuse of Drugs Act 1975. In 2013, legislation was enacted that enables for product approvals related to psychoactive substances, provided that an applicant can show that a particular substance is of a low risk to users. However, although the necessary regulations to implement the legislation are in effect, an amendment to the legislation in 2014 that prohibits consideration of the results of animal testing of substances means that there are currently no approved psychoactive substances or products. Personal possession of a psychoactive substance that has not been approved is an infringement offense, with a NZ$300 fee imposed through infringement notices issued by police.

I. Introduction

New Zealand classifies various drugs and penalizes their cultivation, sale, possession, and use under the Misuse of Drugs Act 1975.[1] The following classifications in the Act are "based on the risk of harm the drug poses to individuals, or to society, by its misuse":[2]

- Class A (very high risk of harm) includes methamphetamine, cocaine, heroin, LSD[3]
- Class B (high risk of harm) includes cannabis oil, hashish, morphine, opium, ecstasy, and many amphetamine-type substances[4]
- Class C (moderate risk of harm) includes cannabis seed, cannabis plant, codeine[5]

Separate from the legislation, the National Drug Policy 2015 to 2020 is the "guiding document for policies and practices responding to alcohol and other drug issues."[6] It is used to prioritize resources and "assess the actions taken by agencies and front-line services."[7] The Inter-Agency Committee on

Drugs oversees such actions and monitors progress against the objectives contained in the National Drug Policy.[8]

Some groups in the country have engaged in ongoing advocacy regarding decriminalizing recreational cannabis use. However, recent reports indicate that there is very little political support for such a change among the parties represented in Parliament.[9] Although cannabis possession remains illegal, with an NZ$500 fine (about US$356) and/or three months of imprisonment applying to simple possession offenses,[10] some offenders may be diverted from the criminal justice system.

One area where there has been a significant shift in approach has been in the regulation of new psychoactive substances, which are commonly referred to as "party pills, herbal highs, legal highs, synthetic cannabis or legal recreational drugs."[11] In 2013, a statute was passed that established a new regulatory system for such substances.[12] The substances can be approved for sale where the distributors or producers prove that they present a low risk to users.

II. Diversion Programs

A young person under seventeen years of age who is reported for possessing or smoking cannabis, where it is his or her first offense and the amount of cannabis does not constitute enough for supply, will be dealt with using options that include a warning, alternative action (diversion), or family group conference techniques. More serious cases are addressed in the Youth Court.[13]

Young people over seventeen years of age will likely be offered diversion for minor cannabis possession or use, especially if it is their first offense. This may involve a donation and/or attending an approved counseling course in order to avoid the court process.[14]

The Police Adult Diversion Scheme may be used for first offenders in relation to a range of offenses, including minor drug offenses.[15] Several criteria apply in determining whether to consider diversion, including whether there is "sufficient evidence and public interest in pursuing prosecution of the case." Generally, this test is not met if it is the person's first offense, the offense is not serious, the person has accepted full responsibility for the offenses, the person has received an explanation of his or her legal rights, and the person agrees to the conditions of diversion.[16] Consideration of whether or not a person is eligible for diversion is undertaken by the Police Prosecution

Service, and the prosecutor will advise the court and the offender if the case may be suitable for diversion.

If the offender wishes to be considered for diversion, he or she will be interviewed about the offense and must take responsibility for it. If approved for diversion, a written agreement will be prepared and signed. Such agreements, and their conditions, are tailored to each individual. For example, they may include a requirement to attend addiction treatment or counseling. Once the requirements have been fulfilled, the prosecutor will "advise the court that diversion has been successfully completed and that the charges have been dismissed."[17]

In 2011, the New Zealand Law Commission completed a report on its review of the Misuse of Drugs Act 1975. Among its recommendations for reforming drug law in New Zealand was the establishment of a mandatory cautioning program for personal possession and use offenses.[18] The report provides information on the key components of such a program, which would essentially replace the Police Adult Diversion Scheme for these offenses. The Law Commission also stated that, if such a program is not implemented, "further consideration should be given to widening the application of the Diversion Scheme to a greater range of personal possession and use offences, including those for Class A and B drugs."[19] There does not appear to be any current proposals to implement either the new caution system or an expansion of the diversion program.

III. Drug Court Pilot

A further recommendation in the Law Commission's report was that the government should consider establishing a drug court pilot.[20] This recommendation was accepted by the government[21] and the five-year Alcohol and Other Drug Treatment (AODT) Court pilot commenced in Auckland in November 2012.[22] According to the Ministry of Justice,

> [p]eople who are selected for the AODT Court and agree to take part will have their case put on hold prior to sentencing to allow them to enter an intensive treatment programme for their AOD dependency (or moderate to severe addiction). This is not an easy option – the programme takes commitment and the defendant will still be sentenced for their crime. If their participation in the addiction treatment programme is successful, this can be taken into account when they are sentenced.[23]

IV. Regulation of Psychoactive Substances

Prior to the passage of the Psychoactive Substances Act 2013, psychoactive substances could be sold in New Zealand without restriction.[24] Due to concerns emerging regarding the adverse effects of such substances on users, the government decided to regulate the substances in a way that allows products to be developed and sold following approval from a government regulatory agency, the Psychoactive Substances Regulatory Authority (the Authority).

A. Background

The first new psychoactive substance introduced in New Zealand was Benzylpiperazine (BZP) in 2000.[25] This substance could be sold legally in the country until 2008, when it was brought under the Misuse of Drugs Act 1975 as a Class C controlled drug.[26] Prior to this, in 2005, synthetic cannabis products had also started being sold. Following the BZP ban, other products started entering the market, leading the 7overnment to place "a series of temporary bans on products that had come to its attention."[2] This process involved identifying the product by its specific chemical structure and led to temporary bans on thirty-five such structures. However, once a substance would be banned, others with different chemical structures would be manufactured, creating a "cat and mouse" game between the government and the "legal high" industry.[28]

The Law Commission's 2011 report on its review of the Misuse of Drugs Act 1975 recommended that "[t]here should be a new regime with its own criteria and approval process for regulating new psychoactive substances."[29] The Psychoactive Substances Bill, which was based on the Law Commission's recommendations, was subsequently introduced in early 2013 and was passed by the Parliament in July 2013, with a near-unanimous vote (119–1).[30]

B. Psychoactive Substances Act 2013

The Act reverses the onus of proof for psychoactive substances,[31] requiring importers and manufacturers, rather than the government, to show that a substance is safe in order for it to be approved. It states that any substance that has not been approved "should be prohibited, on a precautionary basis, until it has been assessed by the Authority and the Authority is satisfied that it poses no more than a low risk of harm to individuals who use it."[32] The Authority explains that

> [l]icences must be obtained by people or businesses who wish to import, research, manufacture, wholesale and retail psychoactive substances and products.
>
> The Act also restricts the sale of these products (when approved) to persons aged 18 years and above.
>
> Before a product can be approved for use, the degree of harm must be assessed by the Authority on the advice of an expert advisory committee and evidence.[33]

In addition to age restrictions,[34] psychoactive products are subject to place-of-sale restrictions;[35] advertising and packaging restrictions and requirements;[36] health-warning requirements;[37] and signage, storage, and display restrictions and requirements.[38] The Authority may, when approving a product, impose any conditions on the approval as it thinks fit.[39]

As required by the Act, the Authority issued a Code of Manufacturing Practice, which came into force in January 2014 and "outlines the quality control requirements for manufacturers of psychoactive substances."[40]

C. Offenses under the Act

The legislation contains three infringement offenses[41] related to a person under the age of eighteen buying or possessing a psychoactive substance, including an approved product;[42] supplying an approved product to a person under eighteen in a public place;[43] and personal possession of a psychoactive substance that is not an approved product.[44] These offenses may be subject to an infringement fee, prescribed in regulations, that does not exceed NZ$500 (about US$356).[45] The fees are imposed by police through the issuing of infringement notices.[46]

Other offenses in the legislation are subject to criminal sanctions. These include knowingly providing false or misleading information in an application for approval of a product, or failing to provide relevant information relating to the ingredients of the product or the effect of the product on those who use it;[47] breaching a condition that has been imposed on an approval;[48] knowingly providing false or misleading information in a license application;[49] importing, manufacturing, or selling an approved product without a license;[50] breaching a license condition;[51] importing, manufacturing, or selling an approved product in breach of any conditions imposed by the Authority;[52] and selling or supplying (or offering to sell or supply) a psychoactive substance that is not an approved product, or possessing such a substance with the intent to sell or supply it to any person.[53]

D. Implementation of the Act

Following the passage of the Act, there was an interim phase during which "a number of importers, manufacturers, wholesalers and retailers were granted interim licences, and some products were given interim approvals, and were subsequently followed up to see if they were meeting their licence conditions and that their products were not causing adverse reactions."[54] In May 2014, amendment legislation[55] was passed that resulted in all approvals and licenses being revoked, and placed a moratorium on processing applications for approvals and licenses until regulations came into force.[56] Therefore, it became illegal to possess and supply all psychoactive products.[57]

Three sets of regulations under the Act came into force in November 2014. The Psychoactive Substances Regulations 2014[58] allow for "product approvals and licences for importing, research, manufacturing, and sale of unapproved psychoactive substances."[59] The Psychoactive Substances (Fees and Levies) Regulations 2014[60] contain the fees for product approvals and license applications, as well as annual levies for holding such approvals and licenses. This includes, for example, an application fee for approval of a psychoactive product of NZ$175,000 (about US$124,675), an annual levy of NZ$88,000 (about US$62,710) for a successful applicant, and a fee of NZ$19,000 (about US$13,540) for an application for a license to manufacture psychoactive substances.[61]

Finally, the Psychoactive Substances (Infringement Fees and Form of Notices) 2014[62] "set out the fee for infringements of the Act (specifically for breaking the age restrictions when supplying, buying and possessing of psychoactive substances, and for personal possession of a psychoactive substance that is not an approved product)."[63] This instrument includes a requirement that the infringement notices state that the fee must be paid within twenty-eight days, and for a reminder notice to be sent out that requires payment within twenty-eight days after service of that notice. If the fee is not paid the person becomes liable to pay a fine and court costs.[64] The infringement fee specified for each of the three infringement offenses listed above is NZ$300 (about US$214).[65]

There are currently no approved psychoactive products. In fact, no applications for product approvals have been received since the full regulatory regime came into effect in November 2014.[66] The Authority's website indicates that this is due to new rules, contained in the 2014 amendment legislation,[67] that "prohibit the use of animal testing for the purposes of assessing whether a psychoactive substance should be approved."[68] The

Authority further states that, for this reason, "it is unlikely that there will be any approved products for at least the next three years."[69]

NORWAY

Elin Hofverberg
Foreign Law Research Consultant

I. Narcotics Legislation

Norway criminalizes the possession and use of narcotics.[1] Norwegian law provides a list of regulated narcotics that includes specific known drugs and unspecified drugs of "similar" effect.[2] Cannabis (marijuana) is on the list of prohibited narcotics.[3] It is currently legal to import drugs containing regulated narcotics for personal medicinal use in limited quantities provided that the person importing the drug has a prescription from a doctor.[4] A prescription drug containing cannabinoids used for the treatment of multiple sclerosis (MS) symptoms is legally available in Norway.[5]

II. Drug Treatment Programs

Violations of drug laws typically result in fines or prison sentences depending on the severity of the crime.[6] However, Norwegian authorities have instituted a program whereby a person can opt to enroll in a drug treatment program instead of going to prison.[7] The program does not make the use of drugs legal, nor is it meant as a legalization effort; rather, it is intended as a program to prevent relapse and additional criminality while improving the health of the person convicted.[8] The program is only available for those convicted of drug-related crimes, such as violations of sections 231 and 232 of Straffeloven (the Criminal Act) or section 31 of Legemedelsloven (the Prescription Drugs Act), or crimes committed while under the influence of illegal drugs or to finance drug use.[9]

The program was first introduced in 2006 and piloted in two Norwegian districts.[10] The project became national on January 1, 2016, and is intended to run at least until December 31, 2016.[11] It provides for routine and unscheduled urine tests[12] and an individualized four–phase program (introductory, stabilization, responsibility, and continuation/transfer phases).[13] Violators of the program are sent to jail.[14]

The program has been criticized by organizations favoring reform of drug laws such as the Norwegian branch of the National Organization for the Reform of Marijuana Laws (NORML) for not going far enough.[15]

Countries with Pending Proposals for Decriminalization

Canada

Tariq Ahmad

Foreign Law Specialist*

Summary

The Controlled Drugs and Substances Act (CDSA), which is Canada's main drug-control legislation, criminally prohibits the possession, cultivation, production, importing, and exporting of certain scheduled substances, including cannabis, cocaine, heroin, amphetamines, LSD, and other narcotics. The use of cannabis (marijuana) for recreational purposes is currently illegal and prohibited. In the early 2000s, bills aiming to decriminalize minor offenses related to marijuana had been introduced but were never passed. The current Liberal government of Canada plans on introducing legislation legalizing and regulating recreational marijuana at the federal level in the spring of 2017.

I. Introduction

Presently, the Controlled Drugs and Substances Act (CDSA) is Canada's main drug-control legislation, with criminal offenses involving possession, cultivation, production, importing, and exporting of certain scheduled substances, including cannabis, cocaine, heroin, amphetamines, LSD, and other narcotics.[1] Certain other drug-related regulations and offenses can be found in the Food and Drugs Act[2] and the Criminal Code.[3]

During the 2015 federal elections, the Liberal Party, which subsequently won the election, pledged that it would legalize, regulate, and restrict access to marijuana.[4] The possession, production, and trafficking of other narcotics will remain illegal. On April 20, 2016, federal Health Minister Philpott announced at a United Nations General Assembly special session on drugs that Canada would introduce legislation on the legalization of the recreational use of cannabis in the spring of 2017.[5]

Currently, regardless of the quantity, possession of cannabis is a criminal offense that results in a criminal record and is punishable by imprisonment and/or a fine.[6] Possession of up to 30 grams of marijuana or up to 1 gram of cannabis resin (hashish) is punishable on summary conviction with up to six months' imprisonment or up to a Can$1,000 (about US$771[7]) fine, or both.[8] Otherwise the possession of cannabis or hashish and other cannabis-related derivatives found under Schedule II of the Act are punishable on summary conviction with up to six months' imprisonment or up to a Can$1,000 fine, or both, for the first offense, and up to one year of imprisonment or up to a Can$2,000 fine (about US$1540), or both, for a subsequent offense.[9] If found guilty on an indictable offense, the person "is liable to imprisonment for a term not exceeding five years less a day."[10] The production of cannabis plants is also prohibited; punishments and minimum punishments depend on the number of plants and whether production is for the purpose of trafficking or if certain factors apply.[11]

Despite these criminal penalties, Canada's youth still have the highest rate of cannabis use among developed countries.[12]

II. Past Proposals

Various bills aiming to lessen the consequences of minor offenses related to marijuana were introduced in the early 2000s. In 2003 and 2004, the Canadian government introduced multiple versions of a bill to amend the Contraventions Act and the Controlled Drugs and Substances Act.[13] In 2003, the Liberal government of Jean Chretien introduced Bill C-38, which sought to decriminalize "simple possession of marijuana."[14] The bill treated the possession of minor and intermediate amounts of marijuana as contraventions under the Contraventions Act rather than criminal offenses under the CDSA.[15] Under the proposal, "[v]iolation tickets would be issued, and existing provincial and territorial systems would be used to process the tickets";[16] an adult possessing less than 1 gram of cannabis resin would be subject to a Can$300 fine (about US$231) while a young person under the age of eighteen would be fined Can$200 (about US$154);[17] and the possession of less than 15 grams of marijuana would only be punishable with a fine of Can$150 (about US$116) for an adult and Can$100 (about US$77) for a person under eighteen.[18]

The proposed legislation would require larger fines if certain aggravating circumstances were present, such as "operating a motor vehicle, committing an indictable offence, and being in, or near, a school."[19] Under those circumstances, adults would be fined Can$400 (about US$309) and youth Can$250 (about US$193).[20] Also according to the bill, the possession of more than 15 but not more than 30 grams of marijuana could either be treated as a contravention liable to a fine of Can$300 (about US$231) or, in the case of a young person, Can$200, or as a criminal offense at the discretion of a police officer.[21] The proposed legislation would also make producing up to three plants punishable by a fine of only Can$500 (about US$386) for adults and Can$250 for young persons.[22]

In February 2004 an identical bill was introduced as Bill C-10 but, like its predecessor, it also died on the order paper without a vote in May 2004, due to the federal election.[23] Another identical bill was introduced in November 2004 as Bill C-17[24] by the minority Liberal government of Paul Martin, but it too died on the order paper.[25] In 2006, the Conservative Party won the election and these bills were not revisited. Therefore, none of these bills have been adopted.

III. Current Proposal

In his 2015 election campaign, current Prime Minister Justin Trudeau pledged to legalize, regulate, and restrict access to marijuana at the federal level in order to "keep marijuana out of the hands of children, and the profits out of the hands of criminals."[26] He promised to "remove marijuana consumption and incidental possession from the Criminal Code, and create new, stronger laws to punish more severely those who provide it to minors, those who operate a motor vehicle while under its influence and those who sell it outside of the new regulatory framework."[27] He also aimed to "create a federal/provincial/territorial task force, and with input from experts in public health, substance abuse, and law enforcement . . . design a new system of strict marijuana sales and distribution, with appropriate federal and provincial excise taxes applied."[28]

Although legislation concerning the legalization and the regulation of marijuana will not be introduced until the spring of 2017, Trudeau reiterated in June 2016 that such legislation will focus on the dual purpose of restricting underage access to cannabis and diminishing the profits of organized crime earned through the illicit marijuana market.[29] The Canadian government has launched a nine-member task force to advise the government on the regulation and legalization of marijuana. In the upcoming months, the task force will consult provincial, territorial, and indigenous governments as well as "youth and experts in relevant fields like healthcare, criminal justice, economics, industry and law enforcement."[30] Companies with expertise in the sale, production, and distribution of marijuana will also be consulted.[31]

The New Democratic Party of Canada had introduced a motion for the immediate decriminalization of recreational marijuana. However, this motion was rejected by the government. Prime Minister Trudeau argues that without regulations in place, the decriminalization of marijuana will result in giving a "legal stream of income to criminal organizations."[32] Until the new law is in place, recreational marijuana will remain illegal.

Plans to legalize marijuana are being complicated by Canada's international treaty obligations.[33] Because the legalization of marijuana may violate such treaties, Canada will have to demonstrate how it plans to conform to its treaty obligations. In some cases, Canada may either have to renegotiate the treaties or formally withdraw from them.[34]

IRELAND

Clare Feikert-Ahalt
Senior Foreign Law Specialist

Summary

Ireland has announced that it intends to take measures to decriminalize the possession of small quantities of illegal drugs as part of its drug strategy. The aim is to remove users, who are typically addicts in need of medical attention, from the criminal justice system. The distribution and sale of illegal drugs will remain an offense. Medically supervised injecting centers are soon to be tested in Dublin, with the aim of taking users off the streets and reducing the incidence of infections among users.

I. Introduction

In November 2015, Irish Minister Aodhán Ó Ríordáin announced that Ireland, as part of its strategy to deal with the country's drug problem, would take measures toward decriminalizing possession, for personal use, of small quantities of such illegal drugs as heroin, cocaine, and cannabis.[1]

Alongside decriminalizing small quantities of drugs for personal use, specially designated, medically supervised facilities would be created for users to inject drugs. The Minister emphasized that the move to decriminalize the use of drugs is a technique to help addicts, in contrast with existing legislation that focuses on shaming them. The Minister stated that he was "firmly of the view that there needs to be a cultural shift in how we regard substance misuse if we are to break this cycle and make a serious attempt to tackle drug and alcohol addiction."[2]

The measures would decriminalize, not legalize, drugs, and the crimes of distributing and selling illegal drugs would continue in force. The shift in focus for individual drug users would be to treat drug addiction primarily as a health issue and remove it from the criminal justice area, which would consequently allow the focus of police resources and court proceedings previously dedicated to users to be focused on drug dealers and traffickers.[3]

II. Legislative Process to Decriminalize Drugs

No legislative proposal or regulations have yet been put forward to decriminalize the possession of small quantities of restricted drugs. One alternative would be a bill to amend the provisions of the Misuse of Drugs Act 1977 that criminalize the possession of controlled substances. Alternatively, regulations could be issued under sections 4 or 5 of the Misuse of Drugs Act to permit individuals to possess small quantities of illegal drugs.[4] Any bill or regulations put forward would have to go through the regular legislative procedure.[5]

III. Policy Considerations

Ireland has studied the system in Portugal, which is understood to have had considerable success since it decriminalized low-level possession of all drugs in 2001.[6] Rising and continual use of illegal narcotics, with little success of addiction treatment under the current system, has led the Irish government to consider other ways to tackle the abuse of illegal drugs. The aim in decriminalizing small quantities of drugs is to remove the stigma from drug users, facilitate the medical treatment and care of these individuals, and reduce the risks posed to them and members of the public when drugs are used on the streets.[7]

In October 2015, Ireland's Joint Committee on Justice, Defence and Equality considered the decriminalization of drugs in small quantities and concluded that drug possession could be handled with civil penalties rather than through the criminal justice system, with the Gardaí (Irish national police service) and health providers having discretion whether to implement these penalties. The Committee also recommended that individuals found in possession of small quantities of drugs be required to attend counseling and treatment sessions to help them stop using drugs, and concluded that further research was needed to ensure that the measures are appropriate to Ireland.[8]

IV. Injecting Centers

As part of a "suite of harm reduction measures," in November 2015 the government announced its intention to create injecting centers where users can take drugs.[9] These facilities would first be established in Dublin,[10] with the aim of opening more in Cork, Galaway, and Limerick. The facilities would be "clinically controlled environments" and users would be medically supervised to help minimize the risks of infection and other diseases.[11] The aim of these centers is to reduce drug use on the streets and its related risks. The government cited research indicating the rooms are "effective in engaging difficult-to-reach populations of drug users. This is especially the case for marginalised groups, such as the homeless, and those who use drugs on the streets or in other risky and unhygienic conditions."[12]

Proponents for these measures believe that these facilities will not only minimize the risks of injecting drugs on the street, but also provide a pathway for treatment, including medical and social care and counseling services.[13] The government hopes that the centers will also allow the government to identify new drug use patterns; the centers "thus could have a role to play in the early identification of new and emerging trends among the high-risk populations using their services."[14]

SOUTH AFRICA

Hanibal Goitom
Foreign Law Specialist

I. Introduction

South African law criminalizes three categories of what are known as "dependence-producing drugs": dependence-producing substances, dangerous dependence-producing substances, and undesirable dependence-producing substances. [1] Offenses relating to "dangerous drugs" (including fentanyl and methadone) and "undesirable drugs" (including cannabis, known as *dagga*, and heroin) are subject to harsh penalties depending on the form of the offense involved.[2] Dealing in any such substances is, on conviction, punishable by a fine and/or a prison term of up to twenty-five years.[3] Use or possession is, on conviction, subject to a fine and/or imprisonment not exceeding fifteen years.[4] Some exceptions apply in both instances.[5]

II. Proposed Changes

South Africa's Parliament is currently considering a proposal to reform the ban on certain uses of cannabis. Legislation introduced in September 2014 seeks to legalize cannabinoids[6] for medical and other uses.[7] The bill specifically states that "no one shall be liable or guilty of any offence for growing, processing, distributing, using, prescribing, advertising or otherwise dealing with or promoting cannabinoids for purposes of . . . treatment . . . and . . . commercial or industrial uses or products . . . ."[8] The bill lacks clarity with regard to the circumstances and extent to which commercial or industrial use would be permitted. Currently before the Portfolio Committee on Health, if enacted in its current form, the bill would accord complete authority to the Department of Trade and Industry to determine terms for the commercial or industrial use of cannabinoids through proclamations.[9] This is reportedly widely seen as a path to legalization and some have called for changes to be made to the bill so that its application is limited to medical use.[10]

End Notes for Uruguay

[1] Ley No. 19172, Regulación y Control de Cannabis, DIARIO OFICIAL [D.O.], Jan. 7, 2014, http://www.impo. com.uy/bases/leyes/19172-2013, *archived at* https://perma.cc/2JDW-P25C.

[2] PITTAMIGLIO, RODRIGUEZ FOLLE Y ASOCIADOS, ABOGADOS, ESTUDIO DE LA LEY 19172. LA DROGA Y SU INFLUENCIA EN EL MUNDO DEL TRABAJO 1, http://www.prfabogados.com/administrador/pdf/DROGA%20%20 TRABAJO%201.pdf (last visited June 29, 2016), *archived at* https://perma.cc/8R47-MCJH.

[3] *Id.*

[4] Ley No. 19172, arts. 1 and 2.

[5] *Informe en Mayoría sobre la Regulación del Cannabis en el Senado Uruguayo-Un Debate Histórico*, TNI (Dec. 10, 2013), https://www.tni.org/es/art%C3%ADculo/informe-en-mayoria-sobre-la-regulacion-del-cannabis-enel-senado-uruguayo, *archived at* https://perma.cc/8V4N-5GPV.

[6] Valeria Gil and Pablo Meléndrez, *Cannabis Legal: Uruguay se Cortó Solo*, EL PAIS (Dec. 11, 2013), http://www.elpais.com.uy/informacion/cannabis-legal-uruguay-se-corto.html, *archived at* https://perma.cc/Q6Z3-UXYR.

[7] *Id.* art. 2.

[8] Ley No. 19172, arts. 17–18(A).

[9] *Id.* art. 18(B) and (C).

[10] Decreto 463/988, Se Crea la Junta de Prevención y Represión del Tráfico Ilícito y Uso Abusivo de Drogas [Creating the Council for the Prevention and Suppression of the Illegal Trafficking and Abuse of Drugs] (also known as Junta Nacional de Drogas [National Council on Drugs, NCD]), D.O., July 25, 1988, http://www.info drogas.gub.uy/html/marco_legal/documentos/ 12-Decreto-463_998.pdf, *archived at* https://perma.cc/TE8X-8KMH.

[11] Ley No. 19172, art. 19.

[12] Decreto-Ley No. 14294, D.O., Nov. 11, 1974, http://www.infodrogas.gub.uy/html/marco_legal/documentos/02-DecretoLey14294.pdf, *archived at* https://perma.cc/CNN5-NMD6.

[13] *Id.* arts. 30–40.

[14] Ley No. 19172, art. 5.

[15] *Id.* art. 28.

[16] *Id.* art. 40.

[17] *Id.* art. 5.

[18] *Id.* art. 6.

[19] *Id.* art. 7.

[20] *Id.*
[21] *Id.* arts. 5 and 7.
[22] *Id.*
[23] *Id.*
[24] Ley No. 19172, art. 5.
[25] *Id.*
[26] *Id.*; Decreto 120/2014, Regulating Law No. 19172, art. 21, D.O., May 19, 2014, http://www.ircca.gub.uy/wp-content/uploads/2014/06/Decreto_reglamentacion_ley_19.172.pdf, *archived at* https://perma.cc/6TAB-VBD6.
[27] Decreto 120/2014, art. 25.
[28] *Id.* art. 26; Ley No. 19172, art. 28.
[29] *Id.*
[30] Ley No. 19172, arts. 8 and 28(B).
[31] *Id.* art. 5.
[32] *Id.*
[33] Gabriel Pereyra, *Casi 5.000 Autocultivadores Registrados y 50 Farmacias Prontas para Iniciar Venta de Marihuana*, EL OBSERVADOR (May 31, 2016), http://www.elobservador.com.uy/ casi-5000-autocultivadoresregistrados-y-50-farmacias-prontas-iniciar-venta-marihuana-n917909, *archived at* https://perma.cc/ZT35-TNP2.
[34] *Id.*
[35] *Id.*
[36] *Id.*
[37] *Id.*
[38] *Sólo 50 Farmacias Uruguayas Comenzarán a Vender Marihuana*, EL DIARIO (June 19, 2016), http://www.eldiario.es/sociedad/Solo-farmacias-uruguayas-comenzaran-marihuana_0_528447402.html, *archived at* https://perma.cc/L6PN-JXMZ.
[39] Ley No. 19172, art. 9.
[40] *Id.* art. 10.
[41] *Id.* arts. 11 and 13.
[42] *Id.* art. 14.
[43] *Id.* art. 15.
[44] JUNTA NACIONAL DE DROGAS and FRIEDRICH EBERT FOUNDATION, EL CAMINO: CÓMO SE REGULÓ EL CANNABIS EN URUGUAY SEGÚN SUS ACTORES POLÍTICOS Y SOCIALES 34–35 (Jan. 2015), http://library.fes.de/pdf-files/bueros/ uruguay/11201.pdf, *archived at* https://perma.cc/JD9N-9625.
[45] *Id.* at 34.
[46] *Id.* at 68.
[47] *Id.* at 69.
[48] *Id.*
[49] *Id.* at 70.
[50] *Id.*
[51] *Id.*
[52] *Id.* at 71.
[53] *Id.*

End Notes for Costa Rica

[1] Ley General de Salud, No. 5395, LA GACETA [L.G.], Nov. 24, 1973, http://www.pgrweb.go.cr/scij/Busqueda/Normativa/Normas/nrm_texto_completo.aspx?param1=NRTC&nValor1=1&nValor2=6581&nValor3=96425&strTi pM=TC, *archived at* https://perma.cc/BT4D-9V4E. The text of the superseded health code, Código Sanitario, L.G., Mar. 15, 1944, is not available.

[2] Ley sobre Estupefacientes, Sustancias Psicotrópicas, Drogas de Uso no Authorizados, Actividades Conexas, Legitimación de Capitales y Financiamiento al Terrorismo, No. 8204, L.G., Jan. 1, 2002, http://www.pgrweb.go.cr/scij/Busqueda/Normativa/Normas/nrm_texto_completo.aspx?param1=NRTC&nValor1=1&nValor2=48392&nValor3=91617&strTipM=TC, *archived at* https://perma.cc/57KH-5QN5. Law No. 8204 comprehensively amended Law No. 7786, Ley sobre Estupefacientes, Sustancias Psicotrópicas, Drogas de Uso no Authorizados, Actividades Conexas, No. 7786, L.G., May 15, 1998.

[3] Ley General de Salud art. 28.

[4] *Id.* art. 127.

[5] *Id.* art. 371.

[6] *Id.* art. 137.

[7] Ley sobre Estupefacientes, Sustancias Psicotrópicas, Drogas de Uso no Autorizado y Actividades Conexas, No. 7093, art. 16, L.G., May 2, 1988, *published in* CÓDIGO PENAL CON ÍNDICE ALFABÉTICO Y LEYES CONEXAS (San José, Editorial Porvenir 1988). A prior drug statute, Ley sobre Drogas Estupefaciented, enacted on September 29, 1930, with an unknown official publication date, is not available.

[8] Ley sobre Estupefacientes, Sustancias Psicotrópicas, Drogas de Uso no Autorizado y Actividades Conexas, No. 7093, *as amended by* Law No. 7233, L.G., May 21, 1991, http://www.pgrweb.go.cr/scij/Busqueda/Normativa/Normas/nrm_texto_completo.aspx?param1=NRTC&nValor1=1&nValor2=4971&nValor3=78293&strTipM=TC, *archived at* https://perma.cc/KQ25-6B6D.

[9] *Id.* art. 24.

[10] Ley No. 8204, L.G., Jan. 1, 2002.

[11] *Id.* art. 58.

[12] *Id.* arts. 3 and 79.

[13] Fiscalía General de la República, Ministerio Público de Costa Rica, Poder Judicial, Instructivo General No. 02- 2010 (Oct. 2010), *available at* http://www.druglawreform.info/images/stories/Fiscalia_-_Instructivo_General_-_02- 2010.pdf, *archived at* https://perma.cc/XFV5-HHNH.

[14] Fiscalía General de la República, Ministerio Público de Costa Rica, Poder Judicial, Instrucción General 01/2011 (Nov. 2011), *available at* http://www.druglawreform.info/images/stories/Fiscalia_-_Instructivo_General_-_01- 2011.pdf, *archived at* https://perma.cc/8PPL-PVMU.

[15] Ley No. 9161, Reforma de la Ley No. 8204 sobre Estupefacientes, Sustancias Psicotrópicas, Drogas de Uso no Autorizado, Actividades Conexas, Legitimación de Capitales y Financiamiento de Terrorismo, L.G., Sept. 23, 2013, http://www.pgrweb.go.cr/scij/Busqueda/Normativa/Normas/nrm_texto_completo.aspx?param1=NRTC&nValor1=1&nValor2=75699&nValor3=93995&strTipM=TC, *archived at* https://perma.cc/C6S9-6EPL.

[16] Proyecto de Ley, Ley para la Investigación, Regulación y Control de las Plantas Cannabis y Cáñamo para Uso Medicinal, Alimentario e Industrial, Exp. No. 19.256 (introduced Aug. 14, 2014, by Marvin Atencio Delgado, Diputado), *available at* http://www.druglawreform.info/ images/stories/Proyecto-19256_Cannabis.pdf, *archived at* https://perma.cc/3MD6-XM63.

[17] Andrés Martínez, *Gobierno Abre Debate en Congreso sobre Legislación de Marihuana Medicinal*, TELETICA.COM (Dec. 15, 2014), *available at* http://www.teletica.com/ Noticias/75247-Gobierno-abre-debate-en-Congreso-sobrelegalizacion-de-marihuana-medicinal.note.aspx, *archived at* https://perma.cc/J84S-946A.

[18] Telephone Interview with Centro de Investigación Legislativa del Departamento de Servicios Bibliotecarios, Documentación e Información [Center for Legal Research of the Costa Rican Legislative Assembly] (June 27, 2016).

[19] *See* Katherine Chaves R., *Siembra de Cannabis Para Consumo Personal No Está Penalizada*, LA NACIÓN (Jan. 20, 2016), http://www.nacion.com/sucesos/juicios/Siembra-cannabis-consumo-personal-penalizada_0_15376 46251.html, *archived at* https://perma.cc/9B7D-P33X.

[20] *Costa Rica: Tribunal Absuelve a Abogado que Cultiva Marihuana en su Casa en Alajuela*, ENTORNO INTELIGENTE (Jan. 19, 2016), http://www.entornointeligente.com/articulo/ 7726536/COSTA-RICA-Tribunalabsuelve-a-abogado-que-cultiva-marihuana-en-su-casa-en-Alajuela, *archived at* https://perma.cc/J955-EJHR.

End Notes for Czech Republic

[1] Tereza Filipková, *Cannabis Policy in the Czech Republic*, TNI (Sept. 25, 2015), https://www.tni.org/en/article/ cannabis-policy-in-the-czech-republic, *archived at* https://perma.cc/3LXC-NG8Y.

[2] Testni zakon [Criminal Law] No. 140/1961, Dec. 8, 1961, SBIRKA ZAKONU [SB] [OFFICIAL GAZETTE] No. 65/1961, http://www.zakonyprolidi.cz/cs/1961-140/zneni-0, *archived at* https://perma.cc/R6DT-KJ45, English translation *available at* http://www.coe.int/t/dlapil/ codexter/Source/country_profiles/legislation/CT%20Legislation%20-%20Czech%20 Republic%20Criminal%20Code.pdf, *archived at* https://perma.cc/4DZ8-BDB4.

[3] *Id.*

[4] Zákon č. 175/1990 [Law No. 175/1990], May 18, 1990, SB No. 31/1990, http://www.zakonyprolidi.cz/cs/1990-175/zneni-0, *archived at* https://perma.cc/6M53-45TG.

[5] Zákon č. 112/1998 [Law No. 112/1998], May 29, 1998, SB No. 39/1998, http://www.zakonyprolidi.cz/cs/1998-112/zneni-19990101, *archived at* https://perma.cc/GT3F-AJT8.

[6] TESTNI ZAKONIK [CRIMINAL CODE] No. 40/2009, Feb. 9, 2009, SB No. 11/2009, http://www.zakonyprolidi.cz/cs/ 2009-40, *archived at* https://perma.cc/5V5K-JD76, English translation *available at* http://www.ejtn.eu/PageFiles/ 6533/Criminal%20Code%20of%20the %20Czech%20Republic.pdf, *archived at* https://perma.cc/BLT3-V96W.

[7] *Id.* § 283.

[8] *Id.* § 284.

[9] *Id.* § 285.
[10] *Id.* § 286.
[11] *Id.* § 287.
[12] *Id.* § 288.
[13] *Id.* §§ 284, 285.
[14] Zakon o prestupcich [Law on Offenses] No. 200/1990, May 18, 1990, SB No. 35/1990, http://www.zakonyprolidi. cz/cs/1990-200, *archived at* https://perma.cc/RAT5-ZS59.
[15] Filipková, *supra* note 1.
[16] Nařízení vlády č. 467/2009 [Government Regulation No. 467/2009], Dec. 28, 2009, SB No. 148/2009, https://www.zakonyprolidi.cz/cs/209-467, *archived at* https://perma.cc/AKR3-PBK7.
[17] Nález Ústavního soudu č. 259/2013 [Decision of the Constitutional Court No. 259/2013], Aug. 13, 2013, SB No. 99/2013, https://www.zakonyprolidi.cz/cs/2013-259, *archived at* https://perma.cc/X4Y2-45NN.
[18] Stanovisko trestního kolegia Nejvyššího soudu č. 301/2013 [Opinion of the Criminal Division of the Supreme Court No. 301/2013], *available at* http://www.policie.cz/clanek/mnozstvi-vetsi-nez-male.aspx, *archived at* https://perma.cc/XZ9T-QYAM.
[19] Filipková, *supra* note 1.
[20] VIKTOR MRAVČÍK ET AL., NATIONAL REPORT: THE CZECH REPUBLIC – 2013 DRUG SITUATION 15 (Sept. 2014), *available at* http://www.emcdda.europa.eu/ attachements.cfm/ att_239732_EN_VZ_2013_EN_final.pdf, *archived at* https://perma.cc/4D4F-VEB4.
[21] CRIMINAL CODE § 287.
[22] *Id.*
[23] Filipková, *supra* note 1.
[24] CRIMINAL CODE § 285.
[25] *Id.* § 283.
[26] *Id.* § 284.
[27] Zákon č. 50/2013 [Law No. 50/2013], Mar. 4, 2013, SB No. 22/2013, http://www.zakonyprolidi.cz/cs/2013-50, *archived at* https://perma.cc/9SRJ-FUWJ.
[28] Vyhláška č. 236/2015 [Decree No. 236/2015], Sept. 4, 2015, SB No. 98/2015, https://www.zakonyprolidi.cz/cs/ 2015-236, *archived at* https://perma.cc/V9Z5-5LGZ.
[29] Filipková, *supra* note 1.
[30] Law No. 50/2013.

End Notes for Mexico

[1] Ley General de Salud [General Law on Health], *as amended through* June 2016, arts. 478, 479, DIARIO OFICIAL DE LA FEDERACIÓN [D.O.], Feb. 7, 1984, available on the website of Mexico's House of Representatives *at* http://www.diputados.gob.mx/LeyesBiblio/pdf/142_010616.pdf, *archived at* https://perma.cc/EA8H-6PYF.
[2] *Id.* art. 478.
[3] Decreto por el que se reforman, adicionan y derogan diversas disposiciones de la Ley General de Salud, del Código Penal Federal y del Código Federal de Procedimientos Penales [Decree Amending Several Provisions of the General Law on Health, the Federal Criminal Code and the Federal Code of Criminal Procedure], D.O., Aug. 20, 2009, *available at*

http://www.diputados.gob.mx/LeyesBiblio/ref/lgs.htm (click on document no. 44 of the list), *archived at* https://perma.cc/5DF6-PNS2.

[4] *Id.*

[5] Press Release, Senado de la República [Mexico's Senate], Aprueban comisiones regular uso médico de la cannabis [Senate Committees Approve Medical Use of Cannabis] (June 15, 2016), http://comunicacion.senado.gob.mx/index.php/informacion/boletines/29226-aprueban-comisiones-regular-uso-medico-de-la-cannabis.html, *archived at* https://perma.cc/WC54-MN37.

[6] *Id.*

End Notes for Netherlands

[1] Wet van 12 mei 1928, tot vaststelling van bepalingen betreffende het opium en andere verdoovende middelen (Opiumwet) [Act of May 12, 1928, Containing Regulations Concerning Opium and Other Narcotic Substances (Opium Act)], May 12, 1928, Staatsblad van het Koninkrijk der Nederlanden [Stb.] [Official Gazette of the Kingdom of the Netherlands] 1928, No. 167, http://wetten.overheid.nl/BWBR0001941/2016-05-01, *archived at* http://perma.cc/B2GM-HG5W, unofficial English translation *available at* http://www.emcdda.europa.eu/topics/law/drug-law-texts?pluginMethod=eldd.showlegaltext detail&id=2142&lang=en&T=2, *archived at* http://perma.cc/ YD3T-6UV4.

[2] *Id.* art. 10.

[3] *Id.* art. 1, para. 1d.

[4] *Id.* art. 1, para. 1b.

[5] *Id.* art. 1, para. 1c.

[6] *Id.* arts. 2, 3.

[7] *Id.* art. 5.

[8] *Id.* art. 8, para. 1.

[9] *Why Are Coffee Shops Allowed to Sell Soft Drugs in the Netherlands?*, GOVERNMENT OF THE NETHERLANDS, https://www.government.nl/topics/drugs/contents/why-are-coffee-shops-allowed-to-sell-soft-drugs-in-thenetherlands (last visited June 29, 2016), *archived at* http://perma.cc/G64S-NCVM.

[10] Aanwijzing Opiumwet [Opium Act Directive], Mar. 1, 2015, Staatscourant [Stcrt.] [Official Journal] 2015, No. 5391, at 2, § 1, https://zoek.officielebekendmakingen.nl/stcrt-2015-5391.pdf, *archived at* http://perma.cc/ RMU3-ZKY2.

[11] Aanwijzing Opiumwet [Opium Act Directive], Mar. 1, 2015, Stcrt. 2015, No. 5391, *archived at* http://perma.cc/ RMU3-ZKY2.

[12] *Affichering* [Advertising] – A; *Harddrugs* [Hard Drugs] – H; *Overlast* [Nuisance] – O; *Jeugd* [Minors] – J; *Geringe Hoeveelheid* [Limited Amount] – G; *Ingezetenen van Nederland* [Residents from the Netherlands – I.

[13] GOVERNMENT OF THE NETHERLANDS, *supra* note 9.

[14] Opium Act Directive, at 6, § 3.4.

[15] *Id.* at 3, § 1.

[16] Opium Act art. 13b.

[17] *Coffeeshops: Toeristen kunnen nog steeds in coffeeshops gebruiken in Amsterdam* [*Coffeeshops: Tourists Can Still Use in Coffeeshops in Amsterdam*, I AMSTERDAM,

http://www.iamsterdam.com/nl/uit-in-amsterdam/ontdekamsterdam/feiten-en-cijfers/coffeeshops (last visited June 29, 2016), *archived at* http://perma.cc/R9M3-9ZSS.

[18] BERT BIELEMAN ET AL., COFFEESHOPS IN NEDERLAND 2014 [COFFEE SHOPS IN THE NETHERLANDS 2014] at 5 (May 2015), *available at* https://www.rijksoverheid.nl/binaries/rijksoverheid/documenten/rapporten/2015/05/01/coffeeshops-in-nederland-2014/coffeeshops-in-nederland-2014.pdf, *archived at* http://perma.cc/Q6VY-B3Z8.

[19] *Id.* at 37.

[20] Opium Act Directive, at 3, § 2.

[21] Richtlijn voor strafvordering Opiumwet, softdrugs [Directive for the Prosecution of Opium Act Offenses – Soft Drugs], June 1, 2016, Stcrt. 2016, No. 23647, https://zoek.officielebekendmakingen.nl/stcrt-2016-23647.pdf, *archived at* http://perma.cc/2GEE-W6V4.

[22] *Id.* pp. 1 and 2.

[23] Richtlijn voor strafvordering opiumwet, harddrugs [Directive for the Prosecution of Opium Act Offenses – Hard Drugs], Mar. 1, 2015, Stcrt. 2015, No. 4953-n1, https://zoek.officielebekendmakingen.nl/stcrt-2015-4953-n1.pdf, *archived at* http://perma.cc/AM8N-38H4.

[24] Wet van 9 juli 2004 tot wijziging van het Wetboek van Strafrecht, het Wetboek van Strafvordering en de Penitentiaire beginselenwet (Plaatsing in een inrichting voor stelselmatige daders) [Act of July 9, 2004, Amending the Penal Code, the Code of Criminal Procedure, and the Prisons Act (Placement in an Institution for Habitual Offenders)], July 9, 2004, Stb. 2004, No. 351, https://zoek.officielebekendmakingen.nl/stb-2004-351.pdf, *archived at* http://perma.cc/P9JK-2SNZ.

End Notes for Portugal

[1] *Política Portuguesa*, SICAD, http://www.sicad.pt/PT/PoliticaPortuguesa/SitePages/Home%20Page.aspx (last visited June 16, 2016), *archived at* https://perma.cc/Y8F6-8M68.

[2] Despacho 3229/98 (2a. Série), DIÁRIO DA REPÚBLICA No. 45/1998, Série II, de 23 de Fevereiro de 1998, https://dre.pt/web/guest/analisejuridica/-/aj/publicDetails/maximized?p_auth=MguOwVr4&p_p_auth=YyURA 4xc&diplomaId=3319678&mode=pdt, *archived at* https://perma.cc/Z5XP-YSGN.

[3] Resolução do Conselho de Ministros No. 46/99, DIÁRIO DA REPÚBLICA No. 122, Série I-B, de 26 de Maio de 1999, http://www.sicad.pt/BK/ Publicacoes/Lists/ SICAD_PUBLICACOES/Attachments/71/ENresolucao.pdf, *archived at* https://perma.cc/8T3N-MCU7; *see also* SICAD, *supra* note 1.

[4] Resolução do Conselho de Ministros No. 46, Item 26.

[5] *Id.*

[6] Lei No. 30/2000, de 29 de Novembro, *as amended by* Decreto-Lei No. 114/2011, de 30 de Novembro, art. 1(1), http://www.pgdlisboa.pt/leis/lei_mostra_articulado.php?nid=186&tabela=leis&so_miolo, *archived at* https://perma.cc/S4VS-4LQR.

[7] *Id.* art. 1(2).

[8] *Id.* art. 28. Decree-Law No. 15 of January 22, 1993 defines the legal framework applicable to the trafficking and consumption of narcotic drugs and psychotropic substances. Decreto-Lei No. 15/93, de 22 de Janeiro, *as amended by* Lei No. 77/2014, de 11 de Novemebro, art. 1, http://www.pgdlisboa.pt/leis/lei_mostra_articulado.php? nid=181&tabela=leis, *archived at* https://perma.cc/E2W2-F5XH.

[9] *Id.* art. 2(1). Decree-Law No. 433, of October 27, 1982, *as amended by* Law No. 109 of December 24, 2001, defines *contra-ordenação* as all illegal and objectionable (*censurável*) facts that fit into a legal category subject to a fine. Decreto-Lei No. 433/82, de 27 de Outubro, *as amended by* Lei No. 109/2001, de 24 de Dezembro, art. 1, http://www.pgdlisboa.pt/ leis/lei_mostra_articulado.php?nid=166&tabela=leis, *archived at* https://perma.cc/7S23 PEW9.

[10] Lei No. 30/2000, art. 2(2).

[11] *Id.* art. 5(1). On January 26, 2012, Decree-Law No. 17/2012 replaced the Institute for Drugs and Drug Addiction with the Intervention Service in Addictive Behaviors and Dependencies (Serviço de Intervenção nos Comportamentos Aditivos e nas Dependências, SICAD). Decreto-Lei No. 17/2012, de 26 de Janeiro, art. 10, http://www.sicad.pt/BK/Institucional/Legislacao/Lists/SICAD_LEGISLACAO/Attachments/818/DecretoLei_17_2012.pdf, *archived at* https://perma.cc/HL79-QKLU.

[12] Lei No. 30/2000, art. 5(2).

[13] *Id.* art. 4(1). Article 8(1) of Law No. 30 determines that the Commission has territorial jurisdiction over the user's home area, unless this is unknown, in which case the Commission where the user was found has jurisdiction.

[14] *Id.* art. 4(2).

[15] *Id.* art. 10(1).

[16] *Id.* art. 10(2).

[17] *Id.* art. 10(3).

[18] *Id.* art. 10(4).

[19] *Id.* art. 10(5).

[20] *Id.* art. 12(1).

[21] *Id.* art. 12(2).

[22] *Id.* art. 12(3).

[23] *Id.* art. 11(1).

[24] *Id.* art. 11(2).

[25] *Id.* art. 11(3).

[26] *Id.* art. 11(4).

[27] *Id.* art. 13(1).

[28] *Id.* art. 13(2).

[29] *Id.* art. 13(4).

[30] *Id.* art. 14(1).

[31] *Id.* art. 14(2).

[32] *Id.* art. 14(3).

[33] *Id.* art. 14(4).

[34] *Id.* art. 15(1).

[35] *Id.* art. 15(2).

[36] *Id.* art. 15(3).

[37] *Id.* art. 15(4).

[38] *Id.* art. 17(1).

[39] *Id.* art. 17(2) (translation by author).

[40] *Id.* art. 17(3).

[41] CÓDIGO PENAL, Decreto-Lei No. 48/95, de 15 de Março, *as amended by* Lei No. 110/2015, de 26 de Agosto, art. 58(1), http://www.pgdlisboa.pt/leis/lei_mostra_articulado.php?nid=109&tabela=leis&ficha=1&pagina=1&so_miolo, *archived at* https://perma.cc/ZLS8-ANF4.

[42] *Id.* art. 58(2).
[43] *Id.* art. 58(3).
[44] *Id.* art. 58(4).
[45] Lei No. 30/2000, arts. 16(1), 16(2).
[46] *Id.* art. 16(3).
[47] *Id.* art. 18(1).
[48] *Id.* art. 18(2).
[49] *Id.* art. 18(3).
[50] *Id.* art. 18(4).
[51] *Id.* art. 19(1). The regime of periodic presentation is determined by an order (*portaria*) issued by the Minister of Health. *Id.* art. 19(4).
[52] *Id.* art. 19(2).
[53] *Id.* art. 19(3).
[54] *Id.* art. 20(1).
[55] *Id.* art. 20(2).
[56] *Id.* art. 21(1).
[57] *Id.* art. 21(2).
[58] *Id.* art. 22(1).
[59] *Id.* art. 22(2).
[60] *Id.* art. 23(1).
[61] *Id.* art. 23(2).
[62] *Id.* art. 23(3).
[63] *Id.* art. 24.
[64] *Id.* art. 25.
[65] *Id.* art. 26 (indirectly referencing Decree-Law No. 433, of October 27, 1982, *as amended by* Law No. 109 of December 24, 2001).
[66] *Id.* art. 5(1).
[67] Decreto-Lei No. 130-A/2001, de 23 de Abril, *as amended by* Decreto-Lei No. 114/2011, de 30 de Novembro, art. 1, http://www.pgdlisboa.pt/leis/lei_mostra_articulado.php?nid=193& tabela=leis, *archived at* https://perma.cc/ 6DMM-RP3X.
[68] *Id.* art. 2(1).
[69] *Id.* art. 2(2).
[70] *Id.* art. 9(1) (translation by author).
[71] *Id.* art. 9(2).
[72] *Id.* art. 9(3).
[73] *Id.* art. 9(4).
[74] *Id.* art. 9(5).
[75] *Id.* art. 10(1).
[76] *Id.* art. 10(2).
[77] *Id.* art. 11(1).
[78] *Id.* art. 11(2).
[79] *Id.* art. 11(3).
[80] Decreto-Lei No. 183/2001, de 21 de Junho, http://www.pgdlisboa.pt/leis/lei_mostra_articulado.php?nid=196& tabela=leis&ficha=1&pagina=1&, *archived at* https://perma.cc/DF9L-4LXH.
[81] *Id.* art. 1.
[82] *Id.* art. 2(1).
[83] *Id.* art. 2(2).

[84] *Id.* art. 2(3).
[85] *Id.* art. 3 (translation by author).
[86] *Id.* art. 6(1).
[87] *Id.* art. 6(2). The management and functioning of the supporting offices are regulated by articles 7–13 of Decree-Law No. 183/2001.
[88] *Id.* art. 14(1).
[89] *Id.* art. 14(2). The management and functioning of reception centers are regulated by articles 15–20 of Decree-Law No. 183/2001.
[90] *Id.* art. 21(1).
[91] *Id.* art. 21(2). The management and functioning of shelter centers are regulated by articles 22–28 of Decree-Law No. 183/2001.
[92] *Id.* art. 29(1).
[93] *Id.* art. 29(2). The management and functioning of points of contact and information are regulated by articles 30– 34 of Decree-Law No. 183/2001.
[94] *Id.* art. 35 (translation by author). The management and functioning of mobile spaces are regulated by articles 36– 41 of Decree-Law No. 183/2001.
[95] *Id.* art. 42 (translation by author). The management and functioning of the replacement programs are regulated by articles 43–49 of Decree-Law No. 183/2001.
[96] *Id.* art. 50(1).
[97] *Id.* art. 50(2). The management and functioning of the needle exchange programs are regulated by articles 51–57 of Decree-Law No. 183/2001.
[98] *Id.* art. 58. The management and functioning of the street teams are regulated by articles 59–64 of Decree-Law No. 183/2001.
[99] *Id.* art. 65. The management and functioning of the programs for supervised use are regulated by articles 66–72, 74 of Decree-Law No. 183/2001.

End Notes for Argentina

[1] Ley No. 23737, art. 14, para. 1, Sept. 1, 1989, BOLETIN OFICIAL [B.O.], Oct. 10, 1989, http://servicios.infoleg. gob.ar/infolegInternet/anexos/0-4999/138/texact.htm, *archived at* https://perma.cc/G78S-55ZU.
[2] *Id.* art. 14, para. 2 and art. 17.
[3] Corte Suprema de Justicia de la Nación [CSJN] [National Supreme Court of Justice], 25/8/2009, "Arriola, Sebastián y otros / Recurso de Hecho" (Arriola Case) (A. 891. XLIV), http://sjconsulta.csjn.gov.ar/sjconsulta/documentos/verUnicoDocumento.html?idAnalisis=671140, *archived at* https://perma.cc/Z25T-PKHS.
[4] CONSTITUCIÓN NACIONAL art. 19, B.O., Dec. 15 1994, http://servicios.infoleg. gob.ar/infolegInternet/anexos/0- 4999/804/norma.htm, *archived at* https://perma.cc/5GSA-2DT9 (translation by author).
[5] Arriola Case at 86, para. 14.
[6] Santiago Safar, El Fallo Arriola: Punto de Partida para la Edificación de una Jurisprudencia Razonable en Torno a la Tenencia de Estupefacientes para Consumo Personal 20 (unpublished seminar paper, Universidad Nacional de La Plata, n.d.), *available at* http://www.jursoc.unlp.edu.ar/documentos/publicaciones/Fallo_Arriola_cambio_jurispr_en_relac_tenencia_persona_Sant_SAFAR.pdf (last visited June 30, 2016), *archived at* https://perma.cc/S6MEXZT8.

[7] *Id.*

[8] *La Corte no Ordenó la Despenalización General del Consumo de Marihuana*, CENTRO DE INFORMACIÓN JUDICIAL (Aug. 25, 2009), http://www.cij.gov.ar/nota-2156-La-Corte-no-ordeno-la-despenalizacion-general-del-consumo-demarihuana.html, *archived at* https://perma.cc/J223-3FPU.

[9] Daniel Gallo, *El Gobierno Definirá la Cantidad de Drogas de Tenencia para Consumo*, LA NACIÓN (Apr. 25, 2016), http://www.lanacion.com.ar/1892519-el-gobierno-definira-la-cantidad-de-drogas-de-tenencia-paraconsumo, *archived at* https://perma.cc/7J9R-E257.

End Notes for Australia

[1] *See Serious Drugs*, COMMONWEALTH DIRECTOR OF PUBLIC PROSECUTIONS (CDPP), https://www.cdpp.gov.au/ crimes-we-prosecute/serious-drugs (last visited June 21, 2016), *archived at* https://perma.cc/9RRP-JXJH; *Drug Manufacture*, CDPP, https://www.cdpp.gov.au/crimes-we-prosecute/serious-drugs/drug-manufacture (last visited June 21, 2016), *archived at* https://perma.cc/B5YF-448S; *Drug Possession*, CDPP, https://www.cdpp.gov.au/ crimes-we-prosecute/serious-drugs/drug-possession (last visited June 21, 2016), *archived at* https://perma.cc/P7AF27WV; *Drug Trafficking, Selling and Cultivation*, CDPP, https://www.cdpp.gov.au/crimes-we-prosecute/seriousdrugs/drug-trafficking-selling-and-cultivation (last visited June 21, 2016), *archived at* https://perma.cc/TP3Z9KYQ; *Importing and Exporting Drugs or Precursors*, CDPP, https://www.cdpp.gov.au/crimes-we-prosecute/ serious-drugs/importing-and-exporting-drugs-or-precursors (last visited June 21, 2016), *archived at* https://perma.cc/DL7R-BNMA.

[2] *National Drug Strategy*, AUSTRALIAN GOVERNMENT, NATIONAL DRUG STRATEGY, http://www.nationaldrug strategy.gov.au/internet/drugstrategy/publishing.nsf/Content/home (last updated Nov. 24, 2015), *archived at* https://perma.cc/Z3EG-WGSR.

[3] *Draft National Drug Strategy 2016–2025*, AUSTRALIAN GOVERNMENT, NATIONAL DRUG STRATEGY, http://www.nationaldrugstrategy.gov.au/internet/drugstrategy/ Publishing.nsf/content/draftnds (last updated Sept. 2015), *archived at* https://perma.cc/WN8X-ZK2N.

[4] *Australian Responses to Illicit Drugs*, AUSTRALIAN INSTITUTE OF CRIMINOLOGY, http://www.aic.gov.au/crime_ types/drugs_alcohol/illicit_drugs/diversion.html (last modified Apr. 30, 2015), *archived at* https://perma.cc/SGJ7 9EDX.

[5] AUSTRALIAN INSTITUTE OF HEALTH AND WELFARE, ALCOHOL AND OTHER DRUG TREATMENT AND DIVERSION FROM THE AUSTRALIAN CRIMINAL JUSTICE SYSTEM 2012–13, at 4 (Bulletin 125, Oct. 2014), http://www.aihw. gov.au/WorkArea/DownloadAsset.aspx?id=60129549012, *archived at* https://perma.cc/A6HQ-CN8M.

[6] Narcotics Drugs Amendment Act 2016 (Cth), https://www.legislation.gov.au/Details/ C2016A00012, *archived at* https://perma.cc/AQ2Q-C8JZ.

[7] Press Release, Susan Ley, Historic Medicinal Cannabis Legislation Passes Parliament (Feb. 24, 2016), http://www.health.gov.au/internet/ministers/publishing.nsf/Content/health-mediarel-yr2016-ley013.htm, *archived at* https://perma.cc/PM6Z-YHE3.

[8] *See Medicinal Cannabis*, HEALTH.VIC, https://www2.health.vic.gov.au/public-health/drugs-and-poisons/medicinalcannabis (last visited June 23, 2016), *archived at* https://perma.cc/Q4ZZ-UQGJ.

[9] *See Terminal Illness Cannabis Scheme*, NEW SOUTH WALES GOVERNMENT, http://www.nsw.gov.au/tics (last visited June 23, 2016), *archived at* https://perma.cc/XME4-MSF5; Press Release, Pru Goward, NSW Welcomes Progress on National Scheme for Controlled Cultivation of Medicinal Cannabis (Feb. 10, 2016), http://www.health. nsw.gov.au/news/Documents/20160210_00.pdf, *archived at* https://perma.cc/4W82-U4JC.

[10] Press Release, Will Hodgman and Michael Ferguson, Tasmania Takes Action on Medicinal Cannabis (Apr. 23, 2016), http://www.premier.tas.gov.au/releases/tasmania_takes_action_on_medical_cannabis, *archived at* https://perma.cc/FYA8-HETN.

[11] *See Medicinal Cannabis in Queensland*, QUEENSLAND GOVERNMENT, https://www.qld.gov.au/health/conditions/ all/medicinal-cannabis/queensland/ (last updated May 6, 2016), *archived at* https://perma.cc/C8SF-CCZK.

[12] *See generally Cannabis and the Law*, NATIONAL CANNABIS PREVENTION AND INFORMATION CENTRE (NCPIC), https://ncpic.org.au/professionals/ publications/factsheets/cannabis-and-the-law/ (last updated Feb. 19, 2013), *archived at* https://perma.cc/9AZQ-ASWG; Jennifer Ogilvie and Katie Wills, *Police Drug Diversion in Australia*, CRIMINAL JUSTICE BULLETIN (NCPIC, Mar. 2009), https://ncpic.org.au/media/1941/police-drug-diversion-inaustralia.pdf, *archived at* https://perma.cc/7KBS-A3V6.

[13] *Cannabis Laws in the ACT*, ACT GOVERNMENT, ACCESS CANBERRA, https://www.accesscanberra.act.gov.au/ app/answers/detail/a_id/1874/~/cannabis-laws-in-the-act (last updated Feb. 22, 2016), *archived at* https://perma.cc/AD75-UDZD. *See also* Drugs of Dependence Act 1989 (ACT) ss 162, 171(1) and 171A, http://www.legislation.act.gov.au/a/alt_a1989-11co/current/pdf/alt_a1989-11co.pdf, *archived at* https://perma.cc/UJQ5-FMCD.

[14] *Simple Cannabis Offence Notice*, ACT GOVERNMENT, ACCESS CANBERRA, https://form.act.gov.au/smartforms/ scon/simple-cannabis-offence-notice-scon/ (last visited June 21, 2016), *archived at* https://perma.cc/EF6Y-8A9A.

[15] *Cannabis Laws in the ACT*, *supra* note 13.

[16] *Simple Cannabis Offence Notices*, ACT GOVERNMENT, ACCESS CANBERRA, https://www.accesscanberra. act.gov.au/app/answers/detail/a_id/1939 (last updated June 21, 2016), *archived at* https://perma.cc/M6AU-LKQH; *Drugs and the Law*, ACT POLICING, https://www.police.act.gov.au/safety-and-security/alcohol-and-drugs/drugsand-law (last visited June 21, 2016), *archived at* https://perma.cc/Q5DJ-EF56.

[17] Drugs of Dependence (Amendment) Act 1992 (ACT) s 3, http://www.legislation.act.gov.au/a/1992-52/19920918- 4655/pdf/1992-52.pdf, *archived at* https://perma.cc/6C7P-AJ5Q.

[18] *Id.*

[19] Criminal Code (Serious Drug Offences) Amendment Act 2004 (ACT) sch 1 pt 1.3, http://www.legislation.act.gov. au/a/2004-56/20050306-16279/pdf/2004-56.pdf, *archived at* https://perma.cc/T8QZ-T2XF.

[20] Crimes Legislation Amendment Act 2013 (No 2) (ACT) pt 9, http://www.legislation.act.gov.au/a/2013- 50/20131210-56740/pdf/2013-50.pdf, *archived at* https://perma.cc/DN23-N2AG.

[21] Henry Belot, *More Than 480 People Fined for Cannabis Possession Since 2009*, CANBERRA TIMES (Aug. 31, 2014), http://www.canberratimes.com.au/act-news/more-than-480-people-fined-for-cannabis-possession-in-actsince-2009-20140825-1082x4.html, *archived at* https://perma.cc/74HG-C92V.

[22] *Id.*

[23] *Id.*

[24] *Diversion Services*, ACT HEALTH, http://www.health.act.gov.au/our-services/alcohol-and-other-drugs/diversionservices (last updated June 22, 2016), *archived at* https://perma.cc/3TDW-JVDS.

[25] *Id.*

[26] Drug Misuse and Trafficking Act 1985 (NSW) s 10, http://www.legislation.nsw.gov.au/inforce/bdc8fe27-fa54-451f-bf3f-eb3c61509c25/1985-226.pdf, *archived at* https://perma.cc/67GC-N23J.

[27] Steven Bolt, *Diversion From the Criminal Justice System*, DRUGS AND THE LAW – HOT TOPICS (State Library of New South Wales, Find Legal Answers, 2015), http://www.legalanswers.sl.nsw.gov.au/guides/hot_topics/ drugs/diversion.html, *archived at* https://perma.cc/77AY-U5LT.

[28] *Cannabis Cautioning Scheme*, NSW POLICE FORCE, http://www.police.nsw.gov.au/community_issues/drugs/ cannabis_cautioning_scheme (last updated June 20, 2014), *archived at* https://perma.cc/J54P-BGJ2. *See also* Press Release, Bureau of Crime Statistics and Research, Cannabis Cautioning Scheme Evaluation (Sept. 23, 2014), http://www.bocsar.nsw.gov.au/Pages/bocsar_media_releases/2004/bocsar_mr_r54.aspx, *archived at* https://perma.cc/6TCZ-BFFP.

[29] Bolt, *supra* note 27.

[30] *Id.*

[31] *Id.* Young Offenders Act 1997 (NSW) pt 4, http://www.legislation.nsw.gov.au/inforce/74ebdba2-1c2c-4c65- baac-25fc44c7ae91/1997-54.pdf, *archived at* https://perma.cc/HH94-HRKA.

[32] Bolt, *supra* note 27.

[33] *Id.*

[34] *Id. See generally For Participants*, DRUG COURT OF NSW, http://www.drugcourt.justice.nsw.gov.au/Pages/ dc_participants.aspx (last updated Jan. 29, 2016), *archived at* https://perma.cc/5M73-GBPL.

[35] Misuse of Drugs Act (NT) s 20A and sch 3, http://notes.nt.gov.au/dcm/legislat/legislat.nsf/d989974724db 65b1482561cf0017cbd2/253504625fd126e769257fbd0022ca10/$FILE/ATT5VPPC.pdf/Repm033.pdf, *archived at* https://perma.cc/BG55-YQSB.

[36] *Id.* ss 20D, 20C(d) and 20E; 2 DEPARTMENT OF HEALTH (NORTHERN TERRITORY), THE BUSH BOOK, ch. 1, "Cannabis and the Law in the NT," http://www.nt.gov.au/health/healthdev/health_promotion/bushbook/ volume2/chap1/cannabis.htm#CannabisandtheLaw (last visited June 21, 2016), *archived at* https://perma.cc/YR9AR2D9.

[37] 2 THE BUSH BOOK, *supra* note 36, ch. 1.

[38] *Other Substances: Illicit Drugs*, NT DEPARTMENT OF HEALTH, http://www.health.nt.gov.au/Alcohol_and_Other_ Drugs/Other_Substances/index.aspx (last reviewed Aug. 2009), *archived at* https://perma.cc/9LP2-8VZJ.

[39] Northern Territory Parliament, Ice Select Committee, Northern Territory Response to Questions on Notice 6 (June 19, 2015), http://www.nt.gov.au/lant/parliamentary-business/committees/ ice/Answers_to_Questions_Taken_on_Notice_NT_Police_Service_Public_Hearing_19_ June_2015.pdf, *archived at* https://perma.cc/YN9ZLRTS.

[40] DEPARTMENT OF JUSTICE, MEDIA GUIDE: NORTHERN TERRITORY COURTS – SUPREME COURT AND MAGISTRATES COURT 8 (May 2011), http://www.nt.gov.au/justice/ntmc/media/documents/Media_Guide.pdf, *archived at* https://perma.cc/8BM4-GZ9J.

[41] *Drug Offences*, QUEENSLAND GOVERNMENT, https://www.qld.gov.au/law/crime-and-police/types-of-crime/drugoffences/ (last updated July 29, 2016), *archived at* https://perma.cc/PPC2-VF2U. *See generally Prevention and Treatment for Alcohol and Drugs*, QUEENSLAND HEALTH, https://www.health.qld.gov.au/public-health/topics/atod/prevention/default.asp (last updated Sept. 29, 2015), *archived at* https://perma.cc/X4PS-TG6D.

[42] Police Powers and Responsibilities Act 2000 (Qld) s 379 ("Additional case where arrest for a minor drugs offence may be discontinued"), https://www.legislation.qld.gov.au/LEGISLTN/CURRENT/P/PolicePowResA00.pdf, archived at https://perma.cc/XX8V-CGRP.

[43] *Police Drug Diversion Programme*, QUEENSLAND POLICE, https://www.police.qld.gov.au/programs/drugs/pddp/ (last updated Aug. 25, 2014), *archived at* https://perma.cc/88DX-VHW7.

[44] Police Powers and Responsibilities Act 2000 (Qld) sch 6 (definition of "minor drugs offence").

[45] Drugs Misuse Act 1986 (Qld), https://www.legislation.qld.gov.au/LEGISLTN/CURRENT/D/DrugsMisuse A86.pdf, *archived at* https://perma.cc/P6JZ-VJW4.

[46] *Id.* s 379. *See also Police Drug Diversion Program*, LEGAL AID QUEENSLAND, http://www.legalaid.qld. gov.au/Find-legal-information/Criminal-justice/Diversion-and-referral-options/Police-drug-diversion-program (last visited June 21, 2016), *archived at* https://perma.cc/2MQF-HZX9.

[47] QUEENSLAND POLICE, QUEENSLAND ILLICIT DRUG DIVERSION INITIATIVE: WHAT DO I NEED TO KNOW ABOUT THE POLICE DRUG DIVERSION PROGRAM? 1 (2013), https://www.police.qld.gov.au/programs/drugs/pddp/Documents/pdp_offender. pdf, *archived at* https://perma.cc/L6JY-PGHL.

[48] *Id.* at 2.

[49] *Id.*

[50] *See* Penalties and Sentences Act 1992 (Qld) ss 15B–21, https://www.legislation.qld.gov.au/LEGISLTN/CURRENT/P/PenaltASenA92.pdf, *archived at* https://perma.cc/DU53-9UJP; Youth Justice Act 1992 (Qld) pt 7 div 3, https://www.legislation.qld.gov.au/LEGISLTN/CURRENT/Y/YouthJustA92.pdf, *archived at* https://perma.cc/SF4C-WQU2.

[51] *Court Diversion for a Minor Drug Offence*, LEGAL AID QUEENSLAND, http://www.legalaid.qld.gov.au/Find-legalinformation/Criminal-justice/Diversion-and-referral-options/Court-diversion-for-a-minor-drugs-offence (last visited June 20, 2016), *archived at* https://perma.cc/G56D-38VW.

[52] Penalties and Sentences Regulation 2015 (Qld) regs 5 and 6 and sch 1, https://www.legislation.qld.gov.au/LEGISLTN/CURRENT/P/PenaltASenR15.pdf, *archived at* https://perma.cc/L6TU-CFB8.

[53] *Illicit Drug Laws*, SA HEALTH, http://www.sahealth.sa.gov.au/wps/wcm/connect/public+content/sa+health+internet/health+topics/legal+matters/illicit+drug+laws (last visited June 21, 2016), *archived at* https://perma.cc/9FXW-B4Z6.

[54] Controlled Substances Act 1984 (SA) s 45A, https://www.legislation.sa.gov.au/LZ/C/A/CONTROLLED%20SUBSTANCES%20ACT%201984/CURRENT/

1984.52.UN.PDF, *archived at* https://perma.cc/N7V7-X2HW; Expiation of Offences Act 1996 (SA), https://www.legislation.sa.gov.au/LZ/C/A/EXPIATION%20OF%20 OFFENCES%20ACT%201996/CURRENT/1996.27.UN.PDF, *archived at* https://perma.cc/FR88-D7UQ.

[55] *Id.* ss 33K(2) and 33L(2); Controlled Substances (Controlled Drugs, Precursors and Plants) Regulations 2014 (SA) reg 15, https://www.legislation.sa.gov.au/ LZ/C/R/CONTROLLED%20SUBSTANCES%20%28CONTROLLED%20DRUGS% 20PRECURSORS%20AND%20PLANTS%29%20REGULATIONS%202014/CURRENT/ 2014.236. UN.PDF, *archived at* https://perma.cc/KL34-LWED.

[56] Controlled Substances (Controlled Drugs, Precursors and Plants) Regulations 2014 (SA) sch 5.

[57] Expiation of Offences Act 1996 (SA) s 16(3)(b).

[58] Controlled Substances Amendment Act 1986 (SA) (*see* Controlled Substances Act 1984 (SA) at p. 82, regarding insertion of section 45A).

[59] *Police Drug Diversion Initiative (PDDI)*, SA HEALTH, http://www.sahealth.sa.gov.au/ wps/wcm/connect/public+content/sa+health+internet/clinical+resources/clinical+programs/ drug+and+alcohol+programs/police+drug+ diversion+initiative+pddi (last modified Apr. 6, 2016), *archived at* https://perma.cc/7MKW-E5LQ.

[60] Controlled Substances Act 1984 (SA) s 36.

[61] *Police Drug Diversion Initiative (PDDI)*, CENTACARE, http://centacare.org.au/service/police-drug-diversioninitiative-pddi/ (last visited June 23, 2016), *archived at* https://perma.cc/XQT9-2SDC.

[62] Tasmanian Government, Review of Drug Use and Service Responses in North West Tasmania 11 (Nov. 2014), http://www.dhhs.tas.gov.au/__data/assets/pdf_file/0009/177534/ Review_of_Drug_Use_in_NW_Tasmania.pdf, *archived at* https://perma.cc/7V69-BB36.

[63] Guidelines for Managing Drug-Related Incidents in Tasmanian Schools 2015–2019 (Memorandum of Understanding Between Tasmanian Police and Tasmanian Schools and Colleges) 12 (2015), http://www.police.tas.gov.au.s3.amazonaws.com/wp-content/uploads/ 2010/06/Managing-Drug-Related-Incidents-in-Tasmania-SchoolsGuideline-MoU-2015-2019-A14.100800.pdf, *archived at* https://perma.cc/2XAF-PKC9.

[64] *Court Mandated Diversion*, MAGISTRATES COURT OF TASMANIA, http://www.magistratescourt.tas.gov.au/ divisions/criminal__and__general/court_mandated_diversion (last modified Aug. 12, 2014), archived at https://perma.cc/TP7T-F6MU. *See also* Sentencing Act 1997 (Tas) pt 3A, http://www.thelaw.tas.gov.au/tocview/index.w3p;cond=;doc_id=59%2B%2B1997%2BAT %40EN%2B20160623000000;histon=;pdfauthverid=;p rompt=;rec=;rtfauthverid=;term=;webauthverid, *archived at* https://perma.cc/5EM8-SGH6.

[65] *Court Mandated Diversion: How to Enter the Program*, DEPARTMENT OF JUSTICE, COMMUNITY CORRECTIONS SERVICE, http://www.justice.tas.gov.au/community corrections/court_mandated_diversion/enter_the_program (last modified May 5, 2015), *archived at* https://perma.cc/E334-SKXE.

[66] *Drug Possession*, VICTORIA LEGAL AID, https://www.legalaid.vic.gov.au/find-legal-answers/criminaloffences/drug-possession (last updated May 11, 2016), *archived at* https://perma.cc/R9DF-N828.

[67] VICTORIA POLICE, YOUNG PEOPLE, ALCOHOL, DRUGS AND THE LAW 6 (2010), https://www.police.vic.gov.au/ retrievemedia.asp?Media_ID=56941, *archived at* https://perma.cc/5ZKQ-TY95. *See also Forensic Services*, HEALTH.VIC, https://www2.health.vic.gov.au/alcohol-and-drugs/aod-treatment-services/forensic-aod-services (last visited June 22, 2016), *archived at* https://perma.cc/3ANG-DPV2.

[68] VICTORIAN DEPARTMENT OF HUMAN SERVICES, EVALUATION OF THE DRUG DIVERSION PILOT PROGRAM 1 (Sept. 1999), https://www2.health.vic.gov.au/Api/downloadmedia/%7BC08C67F6-2B39-4C1B-931D405C66C1C2CD%7D, *archived at* https://perma.cc/8WMB-A8BW.

[69] Drugs, Poisons and Controlled Substances Act 1981 (Vic) ss 73 and 75, http://www.legislation.vic.gov.au/domino/Web_Notes/LDMS/LTObject_Store/LTObjSt1.nsf/DDE300B846EED9C7CA257616000A3571/0D638BDD269A209FCA257761001BFAB9/$FILE/81-9719a084.pdf, *archived at* https://perma.cc/Q6L3-SAJJ.

[70] EVALUATION OF THE DRUG DIVERSION PILOT PROGRAM, *supra* note 68, at 1.

[71] *Forensic Services*, *supra* note 67.

[72] YOUNG PEOPLE, ALCOHOL, DRUGS AND THE LAW, *supra* note 67, at 6.

[73] *Id.* at 7.

[74] *Forensic Services*, *supra* note 67.

[75] Cannabis Control Act 2003 (WA), https://www.slp.wa.gov.au/pco/prod/FileStore.nsf/Documents/MRDocument:4797P/$FILE/CannbsContrlAct2003_00-00-02.pdf?OpenElement, *archived at* https://perma.cc/4VCU8XQY.

[76] Cannabis Law Reform Act 2010 (WA), https://www.slp.wa.gov.au/pco/prod/FileStore.nsf/Documents/MRDocument:20280P/$FILE/Cannabis%20Law%20Reform%20Act%202010%20-%20%5B00-00-01%5D.pdf?OpenElement, *archived at* https://perma.cc/HQ53-PPGL.

[77] *Illicit Drugs and the Law*, WESTERN AUSTRALIA POLICE, https://www.police.wa.gov.au/Your-Safety/Alcohol-anddrugs/Illicit-drugs-and-the-law (last updated Nov. 5, 2015), *archived at* https://perma.cc/DMS7-AD4N. *See also Drugs and Alcohol: The Law*, GOVERNMENT OF WESTERN AUSTRALIA DRUG AND ALCOHOL OFFICE, http://www.dao.health.wa.gov.au/Drugsandalcohol/Thelaw.aspx (last updated July 15, 2014), *archived at* https://perma.cc/6R57-WGWL.

[78] GOVERNMENT OF WESTERN AUSTRALIA DRUG AND ALCOHOL OFFICE, CANNABIS LAWS IN WESTERN AUSTRALIA 4 (2011), http://www.dao.health.wa.gov.au/DesktopModules/Bring2mind/DMX/Download.aspx?Command=Core_Download&EntryId=521&PortalId=0&TabId=211, *archived at* https://perma.cc/243V-2U5A.

[79] *Id.*

[80] *Id.* at 3.

[81] Misuse of Drugs Act 1981 (WA) pt IIIA. https://www.slp.wa.gov.au/pco/prod/FileStore.nsf/Documents/MRDocument:28280P/$FILE/Misuse%20Of%20Drugs%20Act%201981%20-%20%5B06-e0-01%5D.pdf?OpenElement, *archived at* https://perma.cc/L3Z5-3H9Y.

[82] Young Offenders Act 1994 (WA) s 25(3)(b), https://www.slp.wa.gov.au/pco/prod/FileStore.nsf/Documents/MRDocument:28405P/$FILE/Young%20Offenders%20Act%201994%20-%20%5B06-d0-00%5D.pdf?OpenElement, *archived at* https://perma.cc/P73R-K3F5.

[83] *Id.*

[84] *Other Drug Intervention Requirement*, GOVERNMENT OF WESTERN AUSTRALIA DRUG AND ALCOHOL OFFICE, http://www.dao.health.wa.gov.au/Informationandresources/WADiversionProgram/OtherDrugInterventionRequireme nt.aspx (last updated Sept. 30, 2015), *archived at* https://perma.cc/94MX-X8KL.

[85] *Drug Court*, GOVERNMENT OF WESTERN AUSTRALIA DRUG AND ALCOHOL OFFICE, http://www.dao.health. wa.gov.au/Informationandresources/WADiversion Program/DrugCourt.aspx (last updated Oct. 7, 2011), *archived at* https://perma.cc/9SMK-A3VU; *Drug Court*, DEPARTMENT OF THE ATTORNEY GENERAL, COURT AND TRIBUNAL SERVICES, http://www.courts.dotag.wa.gov.au/D/drug_court.aspx?uid=5227-1163-1055-5774 (last updated Sept. 1, 2015), *archived at* https://perma.cc/WF4Q-L7KH.

[86] *WA Diversion Program*, GOVERNMENT OF WESTERN AUSTRALIA DRUG AND ALCOHOL OFFICE, http://www.dao.health.wa.gov.au/Informationandresources/WA DiversionProgram.aspx (last updated July 6, 2015), *archived at* https://perma.cc/MQ64-8FWF.

End Notes for Brazil

[1] Lei No. 11.343, de 23 de Agosto de 2006, http://www.planalto.gov.br/ccivil_03/_ato2004-2006/2006/lei/ l11343.htm, *archived at* https://perma.cc/TP4Y-HHTJ. Law No. 11,343 defines a "drugs" as substances or products that can cause addiction, as specified by law or in lists periodically updated by the federal executive branch of the government. *Id.* art. 1 (sole para.).

[2] *Id.* art. 28. The penalties provided for in sections II and III of article 28 must be applied for a maximum of five months. *Id.* art. 28(§ 3). In the case of recidivism, the penalties provided for in sections II and III of article 28 must be applied for a maximum of ten months. *Id.* art. 28(§ 4).

[3] *Id.* art. 28(§ 1).

[4] *Id.* art. 28(§ 2).

[5] *Id.* art. 33.

[6] According to article 102(III) of the Brazilian Constitution, the STF has jurisdiction to decide extraordinary appeals in cases decided in the sole or last instances, when the appealed decision (a) is contrary to a provision of the Constitution, (b) declares a treaty or a federal law unconstitutional, (c) upholds a law or act of local government challenged as an infringement of the Constitution, or (d) upholds a local law challenged as contrary to federal law. CONSTITUIÇÃO FEDERAL, http://www.planalto.gov.br/ccivil_03/constituicao/ constituicaocompilado.htm, *archived at* https://perma.cc/G36G-5DBR.

[7] STF, Recurso Extraordinário No. 635569, http://www.stf.jus.br/portal/ processo/verProcessoAndamento.asp?incidente=4034145, *archived at* https://perma.cc/CPU2-Q7TG. Article 5(X) of the Constitution determines that personal intimacy, private life, honor and reputation are inviolable, guaranteeing the right to compensation for pecuniary or moral damages resulting from the violation thereof. CONSTITUIÇÃO FEDERAL art. 5(X).

[8] *Projeto de Lei 7663/2010*, CÂMARA DOS DEPUTADOS, http://www.camara.gov. br/proposicoesWeb/fichadetramitacao?idProposicao=483808, *archived at* https://perma.cc/7QQB-EVKR.

[9] *Projeto de Lei da Câmara No. 37, de 2013*, SENADO FEDERAL, http://www25.senado.leg.br/web/atividade/ materias/-/materia/113035, *archived at* https://perma.cc/DBW2-F3MR.

End Notes for Germany

[1] Gesetz über den Verkehr mit Betäubungsmitteln (Betäubungsmittelgesetz - BtMG) [Narcotic Drugs Act], as promulgated on Mar. 1, 1994, BUNDESGESETZBLATT [BGBL.] [FEDERAL LAW GAZETTE] I at 358, § 1, para. 1, http://www.gesetze-im-internet.de/bundesrecht/btmg_1981/gesamt.pdf, *archived at* http://perma.cc/7D9X-FJ7J, unofficial English translation *available at* http://www.bmg.bund.de/fileadmin/dateien/Downloads/Gesetze_und_Verordnungen/GuV/N/Narcotic_Drugs_18_12_2009.pdf, *archived at* http://perma.cc/6HRN-CHP6 (English translation only current to 2009).

[2] DEUTSCHER BUNDESTAG: DRUCKSACHEN UND PROTOKOLLE [BT-DRS.] 8/3551 at 24, http://dipbt.bundestag.de/doc/btd/08/035/0803551.pdf, *archived at* http://perma.cc/TQB6-MEGJ.

[3] Narcotic Drugs Act § 3.

[4] *Id.* § 3, para. 2.

[5] *Id.* § 3, para. 1.

[6] *Id.* § 4.

[7] *Id.* § 10a.

[8] *Id.* § 10a, para. 1, sentence 1.

[9] Berlin – Verordnung über die Erteilung einer Erlaubnis für den Betrieb von Drogenkonsumräumen [Berlin – Regulation on Licensing for the Operation of Drug Consumption Rooms], Dec. 10, 2002, GESETZ- UND VERORDNUNGSBLATT FÜR BERLIN [BLN GVBL.] [BERLIN GAZETTE OF LAWS AND ORDINANCES] 366; Hamburg – Verordnung über die Erteilung einer Erlaubnis für den Betrieb von Drogenkonsumräumen [Hamburg – Regulation on Licensing for the Operation of Drug Consumption Rooms], Apr. 25, 2000, GESETZ- UND VERORDNUNGSBLATT FÜR HAMBURG [HMB GVBL.] [HAMBURG GAZETTE OF LAWS AND ORDINANCES], No. 15, at 83, http://www.luewu. de/gvbl/2000/15.pdf, *archived at* http://perma.cc/43ZS-6J9R; Hesse – Verordnung über die Erteilung einer Erlaubnis für den Betrieb von Drogenkonsumräumen [Hesse – Regulation on Licensing for the Operation of Drug Consumption Rooms], Sept. 10, 2001, GESETZ- UND VERORDNUNGSBLATT FÜR HESSEN [HE GVBL.] [HESSE GAZETTE OF LAWS AND ORDINANCES] 387, http://starweb.hessen.de/starweb/LIS/gvbl.htm (select year 2001 and no. 21 from the menu), *archived at* http://perma.cc/8TXW-H57V; Niedersachsen – Verordnung über die Erlaubnisvoraussetzungen für den Betrieb von Drogenkonsumräumen [Lower Saxony – Regulation on the Requirements for the Operation of Drug Consumption Rooms], Mar. 6, 2002, NIEDERSÄCHSISCHES GESETZ- UND VERORDNUNGSBLATT [NDS. GVBL.] [LOWER SAXONY GAZETTE OF LAWS AND ORDINANCES] 82; Nordrhein-Westfalen – Verordnung über die Erteilung einer Erlaubnis für den Betrieb von Drogenkonsumräumen [North Rhine-Westphalia – Regulation on Licensing for the Operation of Drug Consumption Rooms], Sept. 26, 2000, GESETZ- UND VERORDNUNGSBLATT FÜR DAS LAND NORDRHEIN-WESTFALEN [GV. NW.] [NORTH RHINEWESTPHALIA GAZETTE OF LAWS AND ORDINANCES] 646, https://recht.nrw.de/lmi/owa/br_vbl_detail_text?anw_nr=6&vd_id=2581&ver=8&val=2581&sg=0&menu=1&vd_back=N, *archived at* http://perma.cc/9D34-5UW2; Saarland – Verordnung über die Erteilung einer Erlaubnis für den Betrieb von Drogenkonsumräumen [Saarland – Regulation on Licensing for the Operation of Drug Consumption Rooms], May 4, 2001, AMTSBLATT DES SAARLANDES [S AMTSBL.] [SAARLAND OFFICIAL JOURNAL] 1034.

[10] Narcotic Drugs Act § 10a, para. 2.

[11] *Id.* § 31a, para. 1, sentence 2.

[12] *Id.* § 29, para. 5, § 31a, para. 1.

[13] Bundesgerichtshof [BGH] [Federal Court of Justice], 33 ENTSCHEIDUNGEN DES BUNDESGERICHTSHOFS IN STRAFSACHEN [BGHST] [DECISIONS OF THE FEDERAL COURT OF JUSTICE IN CRIMINAL MATTERS] 8, 14 et seq.

[14] Bundesverfassungsgericht [BVerfG] [Federal Constitutional Court], 90 ENTSCHEIDUNGEN DES BUNDESVERFASSUNGSGERICHTS [BVERFGE] [DECISIONS OF THE FEDERAL CONSTITUTIONAL COURT] 145, 190.

[15] *See, e.g.*, guidelines issued in Rhineland Palatinate: Richtlinien zur Anwendung von § 31 a des Betäubungsmittelgesetzes in Betäubungsmittelsachen betreffend Haschisch und Marihuana [Guidelines to Implement § 31a of the Narcotic Drugs Act for Narcotics Cases Involving Hashish and Marijuana], Jan. 20, 2012, JUSTIZBLATT RHEINLAND-PFALZ [JBL. RHPF.] [OFFICIAL JOURNAL OF THE MINISTRY OF JUSTICE OF RHINELAND-PALATINATE] at 9, https://jm.rlp.de/fileadmin/mjv/Justizblatt/2012/02-2012.pdf, *archived at* http://perma.cc/6PCLSBKM.

End Notes for Israel

[1] Dangerous Drugs Ordinance (New Version), 5733-1973, § 11, 3 LAWS OF THE STATE OF ISRAEL 5 (1981), *as amended*.

[2] *Id.* § 12.

[3] *Id.* First Schedule.

[4] *Id.* § 7(c); Penal Law, 5733-1977, § 61(a)(4), SEFER HAHUKIM [SH] [BOOK OF LAWS] (official gazette) 5733 No. 864 p. 226, *as amended*.

[5] *Id.* § 7(d).

[6] Attorney General Directive, Prosecution Policy – Drugs: Possession and Use for Personal Consumption § 7(b), Directive No. 4.1105 (51.056) (Dec. 1, 1985, updated on Sept. 14, 2003), http://index.justice.gov.il/Units/YoezMespati/HanchayotNew/Seven/41105.pdf (in Hebrew), *archived at* https://perma.cc/B4US-V8V9.

[7] *Id.* § 7(c).

[8] *Id.*

[9] National Authority for Fighting Drugs and Misuse of Alcohol Law, 5748-1988, SH 5748 No. 1252 p. 90.

[10] *Israel Anti-Drug Authority*, IADA, http://www.antidrugs.org.il/english/template/default.aspx?catid=248 (last visited June 21, 2016), *archived at* https://perma.cc/RJF8-Q3ZL.

[11] *Legalization and Decriminalization*, IADA, http://www.antidrugs.org.il/template/default.aspx?catid=109 (in Hebrew; last visited June 21, 2016), *archived at* https://perma.cc/FY3B-CLTL (translation by author).

[12] *Id.*

[13] Private Member Bills for Preliminary Hearing, http://knesset.gov.il/privatelaw/Plaw_display.asp?lawtp=1 (in Hebrew; last visited June 22, 2016) (use סמים מסוכנים [dangerous drugs] as a search term in middle box at top of page; for text of bills, click on any listed bill), *archived at* https://perma.cc/SZ6R-Q4T4.

[14] *Sharren Haskel*, THE KNESSET, http://www.knesset.gov.il/mk/eng/mk_eng.asp?mk_individual_id_t=950 (last visited June 22, 2016), *archived at* https://perma.cc/B9UL-XTZF.

[15]*Dov Khenin*, THE KNESSET, http://www.knesset.gov.il/mk/eng/mk_eng.asp?mk_individual_id_t=780 (last visited June 22, 2016), *archived at* https://perma.cc/A5ZD-DC66.

[16]Dangerous Drugs Ordinance (Possession or Use for Personal Consumption of a Drug Containing Cannabis or Cannabis Resin) Private Member Draft Bill No. 3020, 5776-2016, § 1, http://knesset.gov.il/privatelaw/Plaw_display.asp?lawtp=1, *archived at* https://perma.cc/9ZUD-CR4X.

[17] *Id.* at 2.

[18] *Id.*

[19]Dangerous Drugs Ordinance (Definition of Cannabis Plant) Private Member Draft Bill No. 2874, 5776-2016, http://knesset.gov.il/privatelaw/Plaw_display.asp?lawtp=1, *archived at* https://perma.cc/4B2E-BJ75.

[20] *Id.*

[21]*See Application for a Permit to Hold and Use Cannabis*, MINISTRY OF HEALTH, http://www.health.gov.il/English/Services/Citizen_Services/Pages/kanabis.aspx (last visited June 29, 2016), *archived at* https://perma. cc/4PN2-UGJJ.

[22]Dangerous Drugs Ordinance (Definition of Medical Cannabis) Private Member Draft Bill No. 2855, 5776-2016, *available at* Private Member Bills for Preliminary Hearing, http://knesset.gov.il/privatelaw/Plaw_display.asp?lawtp=1, *archived at* https://perma.cc/R2R6-JH2X.

[23]*Id.* at 1 (translation by author).

[24]Dangerous Drugs Ordinance (Industrial Strains of Cannabis) Private Member Draft Bill No. 2688, 5776-2016, http://knesset.gov.il/privatelaw/Plaw_display.asp?lawtp=1, *archived at* https://perma.cc/ZHU9-84KW.

[25] *Id.*

End Notes for New Zealand

[1] Misuse of Drugs Act 1975, http://www.legislation.govt.nz/act/public/1975/0116/latest/whole.html, *archived at* https://perma.cc/D94E-KNEC.

[2] *Id.* s 3A.

[3] *Id.* sch 1.

[4] *Id.* sch 2.

[5] *Id.* sch 3. *See also Illicit Drugs – Offences and Penalties*, NEW ZEALAND POLICE, http://www.police.govt.nz/advice/drugs-and-alcohol/illicit-drugs-offences-and-penalties (last visited June 27, 2016), *archived at* https://perma.cc/XU8D-283N.

[6] *National Drug Police 2015 to 2020*, MINISTRY OF HEALTH, http://www.health.govt.nz/publication/national-drugpolicy-2015-2020 (last updated Sept. 7, 2015), *archived at* https://perma.cc/5JVP-VSJL.

[7] *Id.*

[8] INTER-AGENCY COMMITTEE ON DRUGS, NATIONAL DRUG POLICY 2015 TO 2012, at 3 (Ministry of Health, Aug. 2015), http://www.health.govt.nz/system/files/documents/publications/national-drug-policy-2015-2020-aug15.pdf, *archived at* https://perma.cc/D72N-EENZ.

[9] Eric Frykberg, *Appetite for Cannabis Decriminalisation Limited*, RNZ (Mar. 30, 2016), http://www.radionz.co.nz/news/political/300255/appetite-for-cannabis-decriminalisation-limited, *archived at* https://perma.cc/7XZW-C4GC.

[10] Misuse of Drugs Act 1975, s 7(2)(b).

[11] *Psychoactive Substances Regulatory Authority: Home*, PSYCHOACTIVE SUBSTANCES REGULATORY AUTHORITY, http://psychoactives.health.govt.nz/home (last updated Apr. 22, 2016), *archived at* https://perma.cc/6495-DRHT. *See generally* Kelly Buchanan, *New Zealand: Psychoactive Substances Bill Proposed*, GLOBAL LEGAL MONITOR (Law Library of Congress, Mar. 5, 2013), http://www.loc.gov/law/foreign-news/article/new-zealand-psychoactivesubstances-bill-proposed/, *archived at* https://perma.cc/2N33-A8LR.

[12] Psychoactive Substances Act 2013, http://www.legislation.govt.nz/act/public/2013/0053/latest/whole.html, *archived at* https://perma.cc/T8BV-L635.

[13] *Cannabis and the Law*, NEW ZEALAND POLICE, http://www.police.govt.nz/advice/drugs-and-alcohol/cannabisand-law (last visited June 24, 2016), *archived at* https://perma.cc/S7EA-92YH.

[14] *Id.*

[15] NEW ZEALAND POLICE, POLICE ADULT DIVERSION SCHEME POLICY 13 (Jan. 2016), http://www.police.govt.nz/sites/default/files/publications/adult-diversion-scheme-policy.pdf, *archived at* https://perma.cc/X7F6-P6BW.

[16] *About the Adult Diversion Scheme*, NEW ZEALAND POLICE, http://www.police.govt.nz/about-us/programmesinitiatives/adult-diversion-scheme/about (last visited June 27, 2016), *archived at* https://perma.cc/6WN8-XEKW.

[17] *Id.*

[18] NEW ZEALAND LAW COMMISSION, CONTROLLING AND REGULATING DRUGS: A REVIEW OF THE MISUSE OF DRUGS ACT 1975, at 30 (R73) (NZLC R122, Apr. 2011), http://www.lawcom.govt.nz/sites/default/files/projectAvailable Formats/NZLC%20R122.pdf, *archived at* https://perma.cc/G2PP-F6CG.

[19] *Id.* at 31 (R79).

[20] *Id.* at 37 (R141 and R141).

[21] Press Release, Simon Power and Georgina te Heuheu, Drug Court Pilot Announced for Auckland (Oct. 19, 2011), https://www.beehive.govt.nz/release/drug-court-pilot-announced-auckland, *archived at* https://perma.cc/6A5VD46X.

[22] *Alcohol and Other Drug Treatment (AODT) Court Pilot*, MINISTRY OF JUSTICE, http://www.justice.govt.nz/courts/district-court/alcohol-and-other-drug-treatment-aodt-court-pilot-1 (last visited June 27, 2016), *archived at* https://perma.cc/Q3ML-E5TR.

[23] *Id. See also Information for Participants: Alcohol and Other Drug Treatment Court Te Whare Whakapiki Wairua*, MINISTRY OF JUSTICE, http://www.justice.govt.nz/courts/district-court/alcohol-and-other-drug-treatmentaodt-court-pilot-1/information-for-participants (last visited June 27, 2016), *archived at* https://perma.cc/3TPA4LBL.

[24] *Background to the Act and the Regime*, PSYCHOACTIVE SUBSTANCES REGULATORY AUTHORITY, http://psychoactives.health.govt.nz/psychoactive-substances-act-2013/background-act-and-regime (last updated Jan. 20, 2015), *archived at* https://perma.cc/PG6X-NAY4.

[25] *Psychoactive Substances Act: Overview*, NZ DRUG FOUNDATION (May 7, 2014), http://www.drugfoundation.org.nz/psychoactive-substances-bill/history, *archived at* https://perma.cc/9624-655P.

[26] Misuse of Drugs Act 1975, sch 3, pt 1, cl 2, inserted by the Misuse of Drugs (Classification of BZP) Amendment Act 2008.

[27] *Psychoactive Substances Act: Overview*, *supra* note 25.

[28] *Id.*

[29] NEW ZEALAND LAW COMMISSION, *supra* note 18, at 23 (R2).

[30] *Psychoactive Substances Bill*, NEW ZEALAND PARLIAMENT, https://www.parliament.nz/en/pb/bills-and-laws/billsproposed-laws/document/00DBHOH_BILL12021_1/psychoactive-substances-bill (last visited June 28, 2016), *archived at* https://perma.cc/DHW8-5Q84.

[31] A "psychoactive substance" is defined as a "substance, mixture, preparation, article, device, or thing that is capable of inducing a psychoactive effect (by any means) in an individual who uses the psychoactive substance." Psychoactive Substances Act 2013, s 9(1). Controlled drugs specified under the Misuse of Drugs Act 1975 are excluded. *Id.* s 9(3)(a).

[32] Psychoactive Substances Act 2013, s 4(e).

[33] *Psychoactive Substances Act 2013*, PSYCHOACTIVE SUBSTANCES REGULATORY AUTHORITY, http://psychoactives. health.govt.nz/psychoactive-substances-act-2013 (last updated Oct. 21, 2014), *archived at* https://perma.cc/3UAR6NUT.

[34] Psychoactive Substances Act 2013, ss 48–51.

[35] *Id.* ss 52 and 53.

[36] *Id.* ss 54–59.

[37] *Id.* s 60.

[38] *Id.* ss 61 and 62. *See generally id.* s 6 ("Overview").

[39] *Id.* s 38.

[40] *Code of Manufacturing Practice*, PSYCHOACTIVE SUBSTANCES REGULATORY AUTHORITY, http://psychoactives. health.govt.nz/industry/code-manufacturing-practice (last updated Oct. 31, 2014), *archived at* https://perma.cc/BM8B-V33G.

[41] *See* Psychoactive Substances Act 2013, s 72.

[42] *Id.* s 48.

[43] *Id.* s 50.

[44] *Id.* s 71.

[45] *Id.* s 72.

[46] *Id.* s 74.

[47] *Id.* s 41.

[48] *Id.* s 42.

[49] *Id.* s 24.

[50] *Id.* ss 25–27.

[51] *Id.* s 28.

[52] *Id.* s 42.

[53] *Id.* s 70.

[54] *Background to the Act and the Regime*, *supra* note 24.

[55] Psychoactive Substances Amendment Act 2014, sch, http://www.legislation.govt.nz/act/public/2014/0024/ latest/whole.html, *archived at* https://perma.cc/88DN-GT2A.

[56] *Id. See also Additional Revoked Interim Product Approvals Information*, PSYCHOACTIVE SUBSTANCES REGULATORY AUTHORITY, http://psychoactives.health.govt.nz/industry/licensees-approved-products/additionalrevoked-interim-product-approvals-information (last updated Feb. 4, 2015), *archived at* https://perma.cc/3E4NFD7P. For a list of interim product approvals that have been revoked or refused, see *Interim Product Approvals*, PSYCHOACTIVE SUBSTANCES REGULATORY AUTHORITY, http://psychoactives.health.govt.nz/licensees-approvedproducts/product-approvals-refused-and-revoked (last updated Mar. 5, 2015), *archived at* https://perma.cc/CJE8- TC9Q.

[57] Press Release, Tony Ryall, Psychoactive Substances Amendment Act Passed (May 6, 2014), https://www.beehive.govt.nz/release/psychoactive-substances-amendment-act-passed, *archived at* https://perma.cc/AY4F-FVBM.

[58] Psychoactive Substances Regulations 2015, http://www.legislation.govt.nz/regulation/public/2014/0243/ latest/whole.html, *archived at* https://perma.cc/X8EZ-YSTD.

[59] *Psychoactive Substances Act 2013*, *supra* note 33.

[60] Psychoactive Substances (Fees and Levies) Regulations 2014, http://www.legislation.govt.nz/regulation/ public/2014/0244/latest/whole.html, *archived at* https://perma.cc/RG7Q-UM3Y.

[61] *Id.* sch 1.

[62] Psychoactive Substances (Infringement Fees and Form of Notices) Regulations 2014, http://www.legislation.govt. nz/regulation/public/2014/0245/latest/whole.html, *archived at* https://perma.cc/JNF9-EAY8.

[63] *Psychoactive Substances Act 2013*, *supra* note 33.

[64] Psychoactive Substances (Infringement Fees and Form of Notices) Regulations 2014, sch (Form 1 and Form 2).

[65] *Id.* cl 4.

[66] *Product Approvals*, PSYCHOACTIVE SUBSTANCES REGULATORY AUTHORITY, http://psychoactives.health.govt.nz/industry/licensees-approved-products/product-approvals (last updated Feb. 4, 2015), *archived at* https://perma.cc/ GPR8-GSWG.

[67] Psychoactive Substances Amendment Act 2014, ss 4, 6 and 7.

[68] *Psychoactive Substances Regulatory Authority: Home*, *supra* note 11.

[69] *Id.*

End Notes for Norway

[1] Forskrift om narkotika (narkotikaforskriften) [Regulation on Narcotics (Narcotics Regulation)] [FOR 2013-02-14- 199], https://lovdata.no/dokument/SF/forskrift/2013-02-14-199, *archived at* https://perma.cc/U889-X3BB.

[2] *Id.* § 3.

[3] *Id.* (scroll down to *Narkotikelisten*, cannabis).

[4] *Id.* § 19.

[5] Press Release, Legemidelverket [Norwegian Medicines Agency], Cannabislegemiddelet Sativex godkjent i Norge [Cannabis Medicine Sativex Approved in Norway] (Nov. 28, 2012), http://legemiddelverket.no/Nyheter/Andre/ Sider/Cannabislegemiddelet-Sativex-godkjent-i-Norge.aspx, *archived at* https://perma.cc/855U-Y7RS.

[6] § 162 STRAFFFELOVEN [CRIMINAL ACT] [LOV 1903-05-22-10], https://lovdata.no/dokument/NLO/lov/1902-05-22-10/KAPITTEL_2#KAPITTEL_2, *archived at* https://perma.cc/WQQ8-YYAY.

[7] Forskrift om forlengelse av prøveordning med narkotikaprogram med domstolskontroll [Regulation on Extension of Trial Period for Narcotics Program with Judicial Controls] [FOR 2016-02-15-152], https://lovdata.no/dokument/SF/forskrift/2016-02-12-152?q= narkotika, *archived at* https://perma.cc/FS5V-ESX2.

[8] *Id.* § 1.

[9] *Id.* § 3.

[10] *Id.* § 1.

[11] *Id.*

[12] *Id.* § 7.

[13] *Id.* § 7, para. 4.

[14] *Id.* § 11.

[15] Ester Nafstad, Op-ed., *Norway: The Emperor's New Drug Policies*, HUFFINGTON POST (Jan. 21, 2016), http://www.huffingtonpost.com/ester-nafstad/norway-the-emperors-new-drug-policies_b_9040746.html, *archived at* https://perma.cc/4NFB-5EE4.

End Notes for Canada

* This report was prepared with the assistance of Law Library Intern Cynthia Chen.

[1] Controlled Drugs and Substances Act, S.C. 1996, c.19, http://laws-lois.justice.gc.ca/eng/acts/c-38.8/FullText.html, *archived* at https://perma.cc/55U6-EKBN.

[2] Food and Drugs Act, S.C. 1985, c. F-27, http://laws.justice.gc.ca/eng/acts/F-27/FullText.html, *archived at* https://perma.cc/FTW7-WBY8.

[3] Criminal Code, S.C. 1985, c. C-46, http://laws-lois.justice.gc.ca/eng/acts/C-46, *archived at* https://perma.cc/ BA3Y-4KUN.

[4] *Marijuana*, LIBERAL PARTY OF CANADA, https://www.liberal.ca/realchange/marijuana (last visited June 29, 2016), *archived at* https://perma.cc/HUK9-6RGY.

[5] *Canadian Marijuana Legalization Bill Coming in Spring 2017, Jane Philpott Announces*, HUFFINGTON POST (Apr. 20, 2016), http://www.huffingtonpost.ca/2016/04/20/canada-marijuana-legaliza_n_9738222.html, *archived at* https://perma.cc/59DY-53ZN.

[6] Controlled Drugs and Substances Act § 4(1).

[7] Exchange rate as of June 3, 2016: Can$1.00 = US$0.77, http://www.bankofcanada.ca/rates/exchange/dailyconverter.

[8] Controlled Drugs and Substances Act § 4(5).

[9] *Id.* § 4(4)(b).

[10] *Id.* § 4(4)(a).

[11] *Id.* § 7(2)(b).

[12] PETER ADAMSON, UNICEF OFFICE OF RESEARCH, CHILD WELL-BEING IN RICH COUNTRIES: A COMPARATIVE OVERVIEW 26 (Innocenti Report Card 11, 2013), http://www.unicef.ca/sites/default/files/imce_uploads/DISCOVER/OUR%20WORK/ADVOCACY/DOMESTIC/POLICY%20ADVOCACY/DOCS/unicef_report_card_11.pdf, *archived at* https://perma.cc/2BBU-7LZV.

[13] WADE RAAFLAUB, LIBRARY OF PARLIAMENT, CANADA'S PROPOSED DECRIMINALIZATION OF MARIJUANA: INTERNATIONAL IMPLICATIONS AND VIEWS, PRB 04-33E (Dec. 17, 2004), http://www.lop.parl.gc.ca/content/ lop/researchpublications/prb0433-e.pdf, *archived at* https://perma.cc/3TK8-F2T7.

[14] Kathleen McIntosh, *Recent Developments in Marijuana Possession Law*, 10 APPEAL: REV. CURRENT L. and L. REFORM 40, 50 (2005), https://journals.uvic.ca/index.php/appeal/article/viewFile/5682/3500, *archived at* https://perma.cc/83B3-HPTY.

[15] *Id.* at 51.

[16] *Id.*

[17] Bill C-38, An Act to Amend the Contraventions Act and the Controlled Drugs and Substances Act, HC 2d Session, 37th Parliament, introduced May 27, 2003, § 5(2) (amending and replacing CDSA§ 4(5) with § 5), http://www.parl.gc.ca/HousePublications/ Publication.aspx?doc=C-38&language=E&parl=37&pub=bill&ses=2&File=16#1, *archived at* https://perma.cc/3GZ6-SSSK. References to Schedule VIII in the provisions can be found here: http://www.parl.gc.ca/HousePublications/Publication.aspx?doc=C-38&language=E&parl=37&pub= bill&ses=2&File=30.

[18] Bill C-38, § 5(2) (adding CDSA § 5.1).
[19] *Id.* § 5(2) (adding CDSA § 5.3).
[20] McIntosh, *supra* note 14, at 51.
[21] Bill C-38, § 5(2) (adding CDSA § 5.4).
[22] *Id.* § 6(2) (amending CDSA § 7 by adding § 7(3)).
[23] RICK CSIERNIK and ROBIN KOOP-WATSON, MANY PATHS TO PROHIBITION: DRUG POLICY IN CANADA, *in* RESPONDING TO THE OPPRESSION OF ADDICTION 320 (Rick Csiernik and William S. Rowe eds., 2d ed. 2010).
[24] *Id.*
[25] NEIL BOYD, CANADIAN LAW: AN INTRODUCTION 55 (2011).
[26] LIBERAL PARTY OF CANADA, *supra* note 4.
[27] *Id.*
[28] *Id.*
[29] Tory Floyd, *Why Justin Trudeau Wants to See Marijuana Legalized in Canada*, YAHOO CANADA (June 10, 2016), https://ca.finance.yahoo.com/blogs/insight/why-justin-trudeau-wants-to-see-pot-legalized-in-canada-163350140. html, *archived at* https://perma.cc/5ZUZ-WEDJ.
[30] Monique Muise, *Canada One Step Closer to Marijuana Legalization*, GLOBAL NEWS (June 30, 2016), http://globalnews.ca/news/2796430/watch-live-feds-to-make-announcement-regarding-marijuana, *archived at* https://perma.cc/FY2P-WJUF.
[31] *Id.*
[32] Joanna Smith, *NDP Urges Liberals to Decriminalize Pot Before Legalizing It*, THE STAR (June 12, 2016), https://www.thestar.com/news/canada/2016/06/12/ndp-urges-liberals-to-decriminalize-pot-before-legalizing-it.html, *archived at* https://perma.cc/9CJR-KY56.
[33] Mike Blanchfield, *Legalizing Pot in Canada Will Run Afoul of Global Treaties, Trudeau Warned,* CBC (Jan. 5, 2016), http://www.cbc.ca/news/politics/trudeau-legalizing-pot-global-treaties-1.3390745, *archived at* https://perma.cc/UNH9-G7Q2.
[34] *Canada's Marijuana Legalization Plan Flouts 3 UN Drug Conventions*, CBC (May 16, 2016), http://www.cbc.ca/news/health/marijuana-legalization-canada-un-drug-conventions-1.3584148, *archived at* https://perma.cc/8A2Y3D6Q.

End Notes for Ireland

[1] Aodhán Ó Ríordáin, Minister of State for Drugs Strategy and Member of Irish Parliament, Address to the London School of Economics IDEAS Forum (Nov. 2, 2015), available on Ireland's Department of Health website *at* http://health.gov.ie/blog/speeches/address-by-minister-aodhan-o-riordain-t-d-to-the-london-school-of-economicsideas-forum, *archived at* https://perma.cc/RMT6-RRMJ; Rose Troup Buchanan, *Ireland to "Decriminalise" Small Amounts of Drugs, Including Heroin, Cocaine and Cannabis, for Personal Use*, INDEPENDENT (London) (Nov. 3, 2015), www.independent.co.uk/news/world/europe/ireland-to-decriminalise-small-amounts-of-drugs-includingheroin-cocaine-and-cannabis-for-personal-a6719136.html, *archived at* http://perma.cc/J5B6-8HR6.
[2] Buchanan, *supra* note 1.
[3] Ó Ríordáin, *supra* note 1.

[4] Misuse of Drugs Act 1977, No. 12 of 1977, http://www.irishstatutebook.ie/eli/1977/act/12/enacted/en/print, *archived at* https://perma.cc/KU7P-MK7B.

[5] *A Brief Guide to the Legislative Process*, HOUSE OF THE OIREACHTAS, http://www.oireachtas.ie/viewdoc.asp?fn=/ documents/bills28/guide.htm (last visited June 28, 2016), *archived at* https://perma.cc/26XC-X9ZD.

[6] Órla Ryan, *Where Do Ireland's Political Parties Stand on Decriminalising Cannabis?*, THE JOURNAL (Ireland) (Feb. 13, 2016), http://www.thejournal.ie/decriminalisation-of-cannabis-ireland-2595145-Feb2016, *archived at* https://perma.cc/ML6Q-KUHX.

[7] Joint Committee on Justice, Defence and Equality Deb., Submissions on Drugs Review: Discussion, Houses of the Oireachtas – Committee Debates (Oct. 14, 2015), http://oireachtasdebates.oireachtas.ie/Debates%20Authoring/DebatesWebPack.nsf/committeetakes/JUJ2015101400002?opendocument#B00100, *archived at* https://perma.cc/GH23-66VW.

[8] *Id.*

[9] Aodhán Ó Ríordáin, Minister of State for Drugs Strategy and Member of Irish Parliament, Address to the CityWide 20th Anniversary Conference: The Way Forward for Irish Drugs Policy – Key Issues for the Next National Drugs Strategy (Nov. 12, 2015), *available at* http://health.gov.ie/blog/speeches/address-by-ministeraodhan-o-riordain-t-d-to-the-citywide-20th-anniversary-conference, *archived at* https://perma.cc/6NJA-B4GV.

[10] Paul Hosford, *Dublin Will Be Getting Its First Drug Injection Centre Within 18 Months*, THE JOURNAL (Ireland) (Dec. 15, 2015), http://www.thejournal.ie/drugs-heroin-injection-centres-2502999-Dec2015, *archived at* https://perma.cc/YRZ7-RQ2B.

[11] Ó Ríordáin, *supra* note 1.

[12] *Id.*

[13] *Id.*

[14] *Id.*

End Notes for South Africa

[1] Drugs and Drug Trafficking Act No. 140 of 1992, §§ 1, 4 and 5, 8 BUTTERWORTHS STATUTES OF SOUTH AFRICA (updated through 2015), version updated through 2010 available on the South Africa Department of Justice website, *at* http://www.justice.gov.za/legislation/acts/1992-140.pdf, *archived at* https://perma.cc/7R3W-KTFP.

[2] *Id.* § 1.

[3] *Id.* §§ 5, 13 and 17.

[4] *Id.* §§ 4, 13 and 17.

[5] *Id.* §§ 4 and 5.

[6] "Cannabinoids" have been defined as "any part or chemical constituent of the plant known as cannabis, marijuana or dagga, any genetic modification thereof, and any extract thereof or product containing it or resulting from processing thereof." Medical Innovation Bill § 1, PMP1-2014, GOVERNMENT GAZETTE No. 37349 (Feb. 18, 2014), available on the South Africa government website *at* http://www.gov.za/sites/www.gov.za/files/ 37349 _gen100.pdf, *archived at* https://perma.cc/2MNY-NS8Q.

[7] *Portfolio Committee on Health*, PARLIAMENT OF THE REPUBLIC OF SOUTH AFRICA, http://www.parliament.gov.za/live/content.php?Item_ID=215&CommitteeID=91 (last visited June 29, 2016), *archived at* https://perma.cc/FE3UUUJ3.

[8] Medical Innovation Bill § 7.

[9] Medical Innovation Bill § 7 and Memorandum on Objectives at 8.

[10] Tamar Kahn, *Weed Out Commercial Use of Dagga, Say IFP*, BUSINESS DAY LIVE (Aug. 13, 2015), http://www.bdlive.co.za/national/health/2015/08/13/weed-out-commercial-use-of-dagga-says-ifp1, *archived at* https://perma.cc/LG4V-NYT9; Russ Belville, *South African Marijuana Legalization May Become Medical-Only*, MARIJUANA POLITICS (Aug. 18, 2015), http://marijuanapolitics.com/south-african-marijuana-legalization-maybecome-medical-only, *archived at* https://perma.cc/3VCH-6CCC; Press Release, The South African Medical Research Council (SAMRC) Responds to the Medical Innovation Bill (May 28, 2015), http://www.mrc.ac.za/Media/2015/12press2015.htm, *archived at* https://perma.cc/JD4H-KKV4; Sipokazi Fokazi, *Dagga Bill 'Would Add to Social Problems'*, IOL (Aug. 13, 2015), http://www.mrc.ac.za/Media/2015/12press2015.htm, *archived at* https://perma.cc/97RR-TXHJ.

In: Narcotics Decriminalization
Editor: Denise Torres
ISBN: 978-1-53610-318-2

Chapter 2

MARIJUANA: MEDICAL AND RETAIL— SELECTED LEGAL ISSUES*

Todd Garvey, Charles Doyle and David H. Carpenter

SUMMARY

In the United States the federal Controlled Substances Act (CSA) outlaws the possession, cultivation, and distribution of marijuana except for authorized research. More than 20 states have regulatory schemes that allow possession, cultivation, and distribution of marijuana for medicinal purposes. Four have revenue regimes that allow possession, cultivation, and sale generally. The U.S. Constitution's Supremacy Clause preempts any state law that conflicts with federal law. Although there is some division, the majority of state courts have concluded that the federal-state marijuana law conflict does not require preemption of state medical marijuana laws. The legal consequences of a CSA violation, however, remain in place. Nevertheless, current federal criminal enforcement guidelines counsel confining investigations and prosecutions to the most egregious affront to federal interests.

Legal and ethical considerations limit the extent to which an attorney may advise and assist a client intent on participating in his or her state's medical or recreational marijuana system. Bar associations differ on the precise boundaries of those limitations.

---

* This is an edited, reformatted and augmented version of a Congressional Research Service publication, R43435, dated April 8, 2015.

State medical marijuana laws grant registered patients, their doctors, and providers immunity from the consequences of state law. The Washington, Colorado, Oregon, and Alaska retail marijuana regimes authorize the commercial exploitation of the marijuana market in small taxable doses.

The present and potential consequences of a CSA violation can be substantial. Cultivation or sale of marijuana on all but the smallest scale invites a five-year mandatory minimum prison term. Revenues and the property used to generate them may merely be awaiting federal collection under federal forfeiture laws. Federal tax laws deny marijuana entrepreneurs the benefits available to other businesses. Banks may afford marijuana merchants financial services only if the bank files a suspicious activity report (SAR) for every marijuana-related transaction that exceed certain monetary thresholds, and only if it conducts a level of due diligence into its customers' activities sufficient to unearth any affront to federal interests.

Marijuana users may not possess a firearm or ammunition. They may not hold federal security clearances. They may not operate commercial trucks, buses, trains, or planes. Federal contractors and private employers may be free to refuse to hire them and to fire them. If fired, they may be ineligible for unemployment compensation. They may be denied federally assisted housing.

At the heart of the federal-state conflict lies a disagreement over dangers and benefits inherent in marijuana use. The CSA authorizes research on controlled substances, including those in Schedule I such as marijuana, that may address those questions. Members have introduced a number of bills in the 114th Congress that speak to the conflict. Additionally, a few marijuana-related provisions were enacted into law late in the 113th Congress.

INTRODUCTION

Federal law classifies marijuana as a Schedule I Controlled Substance.[1] As a result, it is a federal crime to grow, sell, or merely possess the drug. In addition to facing the prospect of a federal criminal prosecution, those who violate the federal Controlled Substances Act (CSA) may suffer a number of additional adverse consequences under federal law. For example, federal authorities may confiscate any property used to grow marijuana or facilitate its sale or use; marijuana users may lose their jobs, their homes, or their right to possess a firearm or ammunition; and sellers of marijuana may lose the tax benefits and banking services that other merchants enjoy, and ultimately their businesses.

Nevertheless, without federal statutory sanction, more than 20 states have established medical marijuana regulatory regimes. Four have gone further and "legalized" marijuana under state recreational marijuana laws.[2] State officials lack the constitutional authority necessary to trump conflicting federal law. Federal officials, however, lack the unlimited resources necessary to trump the impact of conflicting state law.

The following is an analysis of some of the legal issues the situation has generated and some of the proposals to resolve them.

BACKGROUND

Federal regulation of the drugs, chemicals, and plants now considered controlled substances began with the Harrison Narcotics Act of 1914.[3] Relying upon its constitutional power to tax, regulate commerce, and implement the nation's treaty obligations,[4] Congress used the legislation to establish a system under which it taxed lawful medicinal use and proscribed abuse.[5]

Little more than two decades later, Congress supplemented the Harrison Act with the Marihuana Tax Act of 1937,[6] explicitly noting reliance on its tax, commerce, and territorial powers.[7] The Marihuana Act replicated the Harrison Act's procedures in large measure[8] and adopted by cross-reference the Harrison Act's penalty structure.[9] It became apparent over time, however, that the Marihuana Act served no real revenue purpose and in fact had "become, in effect, solely a criminal law imposing sanctions upon persons who [sold], acquire[d], or possess[ed] marihuana."[10]

This proved problematic when, in the late 1960s, the Supreme Court pointed out the Fifth Amendment difficulties inherent in a tax-based enforcement structure like that of the Harrison and Marihuana Tax Acts. The Court in *Marchetti* observed that a gambler's "obligations to register and to pay the [federal] occupational tax created ... real and appreciable ... hazards of self-incrimination" under federal and state anti-gambling laws.[11] The same day, in *Haynes,* it held that by the same token "the constitutional privilege against self-incrimination provides a full defense to prosecutions either for failure to register a firearm ... or for possession of an unregistered firearm" under the tax-based structure of the National Firearms Act.[12] Finally, in *Leahy*, it struck closer to home. There, it held that the Fifth Amendment privilege against self-incrimination provided a full defense to a charge of transporting marijuana acquired without paying the Marihuana Tax Act transfer tax.[13]

Within months, the Senate Judiciary Committee reported out a Commerce Clause/treaty-based controlled substances proposal that featured most of the components ultimately found in the Controlled Substances Act.[14] It classified marijuana with the most tightly regulated substances in Schedule I, but punished its abuse less severely, explaining in its critique of an earlier proposal that

> [T]o impose the same high mandatory minimum penalties for marihuana-related offenses as for LSD and heroin offenses is inequitable in the face of a considerable amount of evidence that marihuana is significantly less harmful and dangerous than LSD or heroin.
>
> It had also become apparent that the severity of penalties including the length of sentences does not affect the extent of drug abuse and other drug-related violations. The basic consideration here was that the increasingly longer sentences that had been legislated in the past had not shown the expected overall reduction in drug law violations. The opposite had been true notably in the case of marihuana. Under Federal law and under many States laws marihuana violations carry the same strict penalties that are applicable to hard narcotics, yet marijuana violations have almost doubled in the last 2 years alone.
>
> In addition, the severe drug laws specifically as applied to marihuana have helped create a serious clash between segments of the youth generation and the Government. These youths consider the marihuana laws hypocritical and unjust. Because of these laws the marihuana issue has contributed to the broader problem of alienation of youth from the general society and to a general feeling of disrespect for the law and judicial process.[15]

Consistent with this view, it called for the establishment of a study commission to examine and make recommendations on the troubling marijuana-related issues.[16] The Commission's final report recommended the legalization of possession of marijuana for private personal use, but that the Controlled Substance Act otherwise remain unchanged.[17]

Controlled Substances Act Today

Congress enacted the Controlled Substances Act (CSA)[18] as Title II of the Comprehensive Drug Abuse Prevention and Control Act of 1970.[19] The purpose of the CSA is to regulate and facilitate the manufacture, distribution, and use of controlled substances for legitimate medical, scientific, research, and industrial purposes, and to prevent these substances from being diverted for illegal purposes. The CSA places various plants, drugs, and chemicals (such as narcotics, stimulants, depressants, hallucinogens, and anabolic steroids) into one of five schedules based on the substance's medical use, potential for abuse, and safety or dependence liability.[20]

Schedule I substances are deemed to have no currently accepted medical use in treatment and can be used only in very limited circumstances, whereas substances classified in Schedules II, III, IV, and V have recognized medical uses and may be manufactured, distributed, and used in accordance with the CSA. The CSA requires persons who handle controlled substances (such as drug manufacturers, wholesale distributors, doctors, hospitals, pharmacies, and scientific researchers) to register with the Drug Enforcement Administration (DEA) in the U.S. Department of Justice, the federal agency that administers and enforces the CSA.[21] Such registrants are subject to strict requirements regarding drug security, recordkeeping, reporting, and maintaining production quotas, in order to minimize theft and diversion.[22]

Because controlled substances classified as Schedule I drugs have "a high potential for abuse" with "no currently accepted medical use in treatment in the United States" and lack "accepted safety for use of the drug [] under medical supervisions,"[23] they may not be dispensed under a prescription, and such substances may be used only for bona fide, federal government-approved research studies.[24] Under the CSA, only doctors licensed by the Drug Enforcement Administration (DEA) are allowed to prescribe controlled substances listed in Schedules II-V to patients.[25] Federal regulations stipulate that a lawful prescription for a controlled substance may be issued only "for a legitimate medical purpose by an individual practitioner acting in the usual course of his professional practice."[26]

The CSA establishes an administrative mechanism for substances to be controlled (added to a schedule); decontrolled (removed from the scheduling framework altogether); and rescheduled or transferred from one schedule to another.[27] Federal rulemaking proceedings to add, delete, or change the schedule of a drug or substance may be initiated by the DEA, the U.S. Department of Health and Human Services (HHS), or by petition by any interested person.[28] Petitions for rescheduling marijuana have been largely unsuccessful.[29] Congress may also change the scheduling status of a drug or substance through legislation.

Penalties

Federal civil and criminal penalties are available for anyone who manufactures, distributes, imports, or possesses controlled substances in violation of the CSA (both "regulatory" offenses as well as illicit drug trafficking and possession).[30]

When Congress enacted the CSA in 1970, marijuana was classified as a Schedule I drug.[31] Today, marijuana is still categorized as a Schedule I controlled substance and is therefore subject to the most severe restrictions contained within the CSA. Pursuant to the CSA, the unauthorized cultivation, distribution, or possession of marijuana is a federal crime.[32] Although various factors contribute to the ultimate sentence received, the mere possession of marijuana generally constitutes a misdemeanor subject to up to one year imprisonment and a minimum fine of $1,000.[33] A violation of the federal "simple possession" statute that occurs after a single prior conviction under any federal or state drug law triggers a mandatory minimum fine of $2,500 and a minimum imprisonment term of 15 days (up to a maximum of two years); if the defendant has multiple prior drug offense convictions at the time of his or her federal simple possession offense, the sentencing court must impose a mandatory minimum fine of $5,000 and a mandatory minimum imprisonment term of 90 days (up to a maximum term of three years).[34] On the other hand, the cultivation or distribution of marijuana, or the possession of marijuana with the intent to distribute, is subject to more severe penalties, ranging from imprisonment for five years to imprisonment for life.[35] Moreover, property associated with the offense may be confiscated without or with any prior or accompanying criminal conviction.[36]

Forfeiture

Either in addition to, or in lieu of, bringing criminal prosecutions, the Department of Justice (DOJ) may choose to rely more heavily on the civil forfeiture provisions of the CSA in order to disrupt the operation of marijuana dispensaries and production facilities. Forfeiture is a penalty associated with a particular crime in which property is confiscated or otherwise divested from the owner and forfeited to the government, in accordance with constitutionally required due process procedures.[37]

Property forfeiture is used both to enforce criminal laws and to deter crime. Forfeitures are classified as civil or criminal depending on the nature of the judicial procedure which ends in confiscation. Civil forfeiture is ordinarily the product of a civil, *in rem* (against the property) proceeding in which the property is treated as the offender. No criminal charges are necessary against the owner, landlord, or mortgage holder because the guilt or innocence of the property owner, landlord, mortgage holder, or anyone else with a secured interest in the property is irrelevant; it is enough that the property was involved in, or otherwise connected to, an illegal activity (in which forfeiture is authorized).[38] Criminal forfeiture proceedings, on the other hand, are *in personam* (against the person) actions, and confiscation is possible only upon the conviction of the owner of the property and only to the extent of the defendant's interest in the property.[39] Property that is subject to forfeiture includes both the direct and indirect proceeds of illegal activities as well as any property used, or intended to be used, to facilitate that crime.[40]

Section 511 of the CSA (21 U.S.C. §881) makes a wide array of property associated with violations of the CSA subject to seizure by the Attorney General and forfeiture to the United States. Property subject to the CSA's civil forfeiture provision includes any controlled substance that has been manufactured, distributed, dispensed, acquired, or possessed in violation of federal law, as well as any equipment, firearm, money, mode of transportation, or real property *used or intended to be used to facilitate a violation of the CSA*.[41] In order to seize the covered property, the government need only show that the property is subject to forfeiture by a preponderance of the evidence.[42] Once forfeited, the Attorney General may destroy the controlled substances seized, and sell the other property at public auction.[43] After expenses of the forfeiture proceeding are recouped, excess funds are forwarded to the DOJ Asset Forfeiture Fund.[44]

Forfeiture proceedings are generally less resource intensive than a criminal prosecution and have been used in the past against medical marijuana dispensaries.[45] In practice, DOJ would be able to seize and liquidate property, both real and personal, associated with marijuana production, distribution, or retail sale facilities, without bringing any criminal action. As explained above, a civil asset forfeiture proceeding is a civil proceeding against the property in question. Although an interested party may object to the seizure, given that such facilities are in clear violation of federal law, so long as the property is indeed being used for marijuana-related activities, it would appear unlikely that many successful challenges to these actions could be waged.[46]

Developments in the States

Most of the states have legislation modeled after the federal Controlled Substances Act.[47] Over the years, some have reduced possession of small amounts of marijuana to a civil offense under state law,[48] while the District of Columbia went a step further and fully legalized possession of small amounts of marijuana and personal cultivation of a small number of marijuana plants.[49]

More than 20 states also have established a state law exception for medical marijuana.[50] Colorado and Washington have enacted legislation authorizing the retail and personal growth, sale, and possession of marijuana under state law.[51] Alaska and Oregon have enacted similar retail marijuana laws; however, they were not fully operational as of the publication date of this report.[52]

Medical Marijuana Laws

State medical marijuana laws follow a general pattern, although most have some individual characteristics and the manner in which they are enforced can differ considerably. Some of their features are attributable to the CSA and a case from the United States Court of Appeals for the Ninth Circuit, *Conant v. Walters*.[53]

Conant, a California physician, sought to enjoin the federal government from revoking his authority to prescribe controlled substances at all in retaliation for his recommending marijuana to some of his patients.[54] Then, as now, the CSA permits the Attorney General, acting through the Drug Enforcement Administration (DEA), to withdraw a physician's authority to prescribe controlled substances upon a failure to comply with the demands of the CSA.[55]

The Ninth Circuit acknowledged the prospect of criminal liability if the doctor were doing more than engaging in an abstract discussion with his patient: "A doctor would aid and abet by acting with the specific intent to provide a patient with the means to acquire marijuana. Similarly, a conspiracy would require that a doctor have knowledge that a patient intends to acquire marijuana, agree to help the patient acquire marijuana, and intend to help the patient acquire marijuana."[56] Yet, "[h]olding doctors responsible for whatever conduct the doctor could anticipate a patient *might* engage in after leaving the doctor's office is simply beyond the scope of either conspiracy or aiding and abetting."[57] On the other hand, such doctor-patient discussions do implicate First Amendment free speech principles. The Ninth Circuit therefore affirmed the district court's order which had enjoined any DEA enforcement action.[58]

As a consequence of the CSA and the *Conant* decision, the state medical marijuana laws are predicated upon a doctor's recommendation, rather than a prescription and the medicine is dispensed other than through a pharmacy.[59] In addition, the laws afford registered patients, care givers, cultivators, and distributors immunity from the consequences of state criminal laws.[60]

Patients

Physicians may recommend medical marijuana only for patients suffering from one or more statutorily defined "debilitating," or "qualifying" medical conditions. The typical list would include the following:

> "Debilitating medical condition" means one or more of the following:
>
> (a) Cancer, glaucoma, positive status for human immunodeficiency virus, acquired immune deficiency syndrome, hepatitis c, amyotrophic lateral sclerosis, crohn's disease, agitation of alzheimer's disease or the treatment of these conditions.
>
> (b) A chronic or debilitating disease or medical condition or its treatment that produces one or more of the following: cachexia or wasting syndrome; severe and chronic pain; severe nausea; seizures, including those characteristic of epilepsy; or severe and persistent muscle spasms, including those characteristic of multiple sclerosis.
>
> (c) Any other medical condition or its treatment added by the department pursuant to section 36-2801.01.[61]

The list usually includes a condition such as "severe pain," or "chronic pain," or "severe and chronic pain" that is easy to claim, difficult to diagnose, and grounds for potential abuse. Some states seek to limit the scope of the term by statute or by regulation.[62] In many jurisdictions, a qualified patient must be a resident of the jurisdiction.[63] Most states and the District of Columbia restrict the amount of marijuana a patient may possess for medical purposes. The limit is usually an amount less than three ounces.[64] Medical marijuana statutes ordinarily do not allow patients to use marijuana in public.[65]

Caregivers

Typically, caregivers must register and be designated by one or more registered medical marijuana patients.[66] Many medical marijuana laws also afford caregivers the same immunity and impose the same limitations upon them as apply to patients.[67]

Dispensaries

Some state medical marijuana laws contemplate cultivation exclusively by the patient or his or her caregiver.[68] Most, however, establish a regulatory scheme for dispensaries.[69]

Retail Marijuana

Four states, Washington, Colorado, Oregon, and Alaska, have established retail marijuana regimes. Each regulates the distribution of marijuana without a necessary medical nexus, but raise many of the same federal-state conflict issues found in the medical marijuana statutes. Much like the medical marijuana regimes, each recreational marijuana regime shares general patterns, but they also each have some unique characteristics. In some instances, for example Washington, the statutory authority establishing the retail regime is fairly specific. In others, such as Colorado, the statute provides only a broad framework while authorizing a state regulatory agency to fill in the details through regulations.

Decriminalization of Personal Possession and Consumption

Each of the retail marijuana laws decriminalizes the consumption and possession of varying amounts and forms of marijuana by individuals at least 21 years of age within the state. The laws, however, prohibit consumption of marijuana in public and maintain a prohibition on driving vehicles under the influence of marijuana, even if it was acquired and consumed in compliance with the state law.[70]

Washington Initiative 502, for example, legalizes marijuana possession by amending state law to provide that the possession of small amounts of marijuana "is not a violation of this section, this chapter, or any other provision of Washington law."[71] Under the Initiative, individuals over the age of 21 may possess up to one ounce of dried marijuana, 16 ounces of marijuana infused product in solid form, or 72 ounces of marijuana infused product in liquid form.[72] However, marijuana must be used in private, as it is unlawful to "open a package containing marijuana ... or consume marijuana ... in view of the general public."[73]

Colorado voters approved an amendment to the Colorado Constitution (Amendment 64) to ensure that it "shall not be an offense under Colorado law or the law of any locality within Colorado" for an individual 21 years of age or older to possess, use, display, purchase, consume, or transport one ounce of marijuana; or possess, grow, process, or transport up to six marijuana plants.[74] Unlike Initiative 502, which permits only state-licensed facilities to grow marijuana, Amendment 64 allows any individual over the age of 21 to grow small amounts of marijuana (up to six plants) for personal use.[75] In similar fashion to Washington's Initiative 502, marijuana may not be consumed "openly and publicly or in a manner that endangers others" under Colorado law.[76]

Oregon Ballot Measure 91 decriminalizes personal possession, for individuals of at least 21 years old, of up to eight ounces of "homegrown marijuana," up to 16 ounces of "homegrown marijuana products in solid form," and up to 72 ounces of "homegrown marijuana in liquid form." It also decriminalizes cultivation of up to four marijuana plants.[77] Ballot Measure 91 also explicitly prohibits "the use of marijuana items in a public place,"[78] as well as the production and storage of marijuana or marijuana products where they "can be readily seen by normal unaided vision from a public place."[79]

Alaska law allows individuals of at least 21 years old to possess up to one ounce of marijuana and six (but no more than three that are mature and flowering) marijuana plants.[80] The public consumption and cultivation of marijuana is prohibited under Alaska law.[81]

Licensing Regime for Retail Production, Distribution, and Sale

Another common feature of recreational marijuana laws is the establishment of licensing regimes for the retail production, distribution, and sale of marijuana. Although the specifics vary, each retail marijuana regime establishes license application processes, qualification standards, and license maintenance standards that are to be implemented and overseen by a state regulatory agency.

Washington Initiative 502 provides that the "possession, delivery, distribution, and sale" by a validly licensed producer, processor, or retailer, in accordance with the newly established regulatory scheme administered by the state Liquor Control Board (LCB), "shall not be a criminal or civil offense under Washington state law."[82] The Initiative establishes a three-tiered production, processing, and retail licensing system that permits the state to retain regulatory control over the commercial life cycle of marijuana. Qualified individuals must obtain a producer's license to grow or cultivate marijuana, a processor's license to process, package, and label the drug, or a retail license to sell marijuana to the general public.[83]

Initiative 502 also establishes various restrictions and requirements for obtaining the proper license and directs the state LCB to adopt procedures for the issuance of such licenses. On October 16, 2013,[84] the LCB adopted detailed rules for implementing Initiative 502. These rules describe the marijuana license qualifications and application process, application fees, marijuana packaging and labeling restrictions, recordkeeping and security requirements for marijuana facilities, and reasonable time, place, and manner advertising restrictions.[85]

The licensing standards in Colorado were implemented through a combination of statutes and regulations enacted to supplement Amendment 64. The Colorado General Assembly passed three bills that were signed into law by Governor Hickenlooper on May 28, 2013.[86] On September 9, 2013, the Colorado Department of Revenue and State Licensing Authority adopted regulations to implement licensing qualifications and procedures for retail marijuana facilities.[87] The regulations establish procedures for the issuance, renewal, suspension, and revocation of licenses; provide a schedule of licensing and renewal fees; and specify requirements for licensees to follow regarding physical security, video surveillance, labeling, health and safety precautions, and product advertising.[88]

Alaska's recreational marijuana law establishes a licensing and registration regime for cultivation facilities, manufacturing facilities, and retail stores.[89] A state Marijuana Control Board is authorized to issue regulations to implement the licensing and registration regime, including rules that establish license application and renewal processes, qualification standards, labeling requirements, and advertising limitations.[90]

Oregon Ballot Measure 91 empowers the Oregon Liquor Control Commission to issue regulations establishing similar licensing standards.[91]

Taxation Authority

Each of the retail marijuana laws also imposes taxes on recreational marijuana. These taxing measures vary in size and applicability and establish different purposes for which the revenue generated through these taxes will be used.

For example, in accordance with adopted regulations, Washington will impose an excise tax of 25% of the selling price on each marijuana sale within the established distribution system.[92] The state excise tax will, therefore, be imposed on three separate transactions: the sale of marijuana from producer to processor, from processor to retailer, and from retailer to consumer. All collected taxes are deposited into the Dedicated Marijuana Fund and distributed, mostly to social and health services, as outlined in the Initiative.[93]

Similarly, Colorado voters approved a 25% tax on retail marijuana transactions (a 15% excise tax that would raise revenues generally to be used for public school capital construction, and an additional 10% sales tax that predominately would generate revenues to fund the enforcement of the retail marijuana regulations).[94]

Under Oregon Ballot Measure 91, marijuana producers will be taxed $5 for each immature marijuana plant, $10 for each ounce of marijuana leaves, and $35 for each ounce of flowers.[95] The revenue generated will be used first to offset the costs of implementing the state's marijuana regime and remaining monies will be distributed to a variety of existing state funds, including the state's Common School Fund and the Mental Health Alcoholism and Drug Services Account.[96]

Alaska law imposes an excise tax of $50 per ounce marijuana for each transaction between a marijuana cultivation center and either a processor or retail store.[97]

Local Control

Another issue relevant to each retail marijuana law is the question of whether local governments within the state are permitted to ban or otherwise regulate marijuana businesses within their local jurisdictions. Colorado Amendment 64 expressly permits local governments within Colorado to regulate or prohibit the operation of such facilities.[98] The Alaska recreational marijuana law also expressly provides local governments with certain authority to ban recreational marijuana businesses from operating and otherwise restrict "the time, place, manner, and number of marijuana establishment operations" with their respective jurisdictions.[99] Oregon Ballot Measure 91 also expressly authorizes localities to impose "reasonable time, place, and manner" restrictions on marijuana businesses.[100] Washington's Initiative 502, on the other hand, does not expressly allow Washington cities to ban marijuana stores from opening within their borders, and there is uncertainty about the degree to which such local prohibitions or moratoriums on the operation of recreational marijuana businesses may be enforced.[101]

Justice Department Memoranda

The Department of Justice is not required, and realistically lacks the resources, to prosecute every single violation of the CSA. Indeed, pursuant to the doctrine of "prosecutorial discretion," federal law enforcement officials have "broad discretion" as to when, whom, and whether to prosecute for violations of the CSA.[102] Courts have recognized that the "decision to prosecute is particularly ill-suited to judicial review," as it involves the consideration of factors, such as the strength of evidence, deterrence value, and existing enforcement priorities, "not readily susceptible to the kind of analysis the courts are competent to undertake."[103]

Through the exercise of prosecutorial discretion, DOJ is able to develop a policy outlining what marijuana-related activities will receive the most attention from federal authorities. Indeed, DOJ has issued four memoranda since 2009 that explain the Obama Administration's position regarding state-authorized marijuana activities, as described in the following sections.

The 2009 Ogden Memorandum

In 2009, Deputy Attorney General David W. Ogden provided guidance to federal prosecutors in states that have authorized the use of medical marijuana.[104] Citing a desire to make "efficient and rational use of its limited investigative and prosecutorial resources," the memorandum stated that while the "prosecution of significant traffickers of illegal drugs, including marijuana ... continues to be a core priority," federal prosecutors "should not focus federal resources [] on individuals whose actions are in clear and unambiguous compliance with existing state laws providing for the medical use of marijuana."[105] The memorandum made clear, however, that "this guidance [does not] preclude investigation or prosecution, even where there is clear and unambiguous compliance with existing state law, in particular circumstances where investigation or prosecution otherwise serves important federal interests."[106] Nevertheless, the Ogden Memorandum was widely considered an assurance that DOJ would not prosecute any marijuana cultivation, distribution, or possession, as long as those activities complied with state law.[107]

At about the same time, it became apparent the state medical marijuana programs had consequences that were perhaps unintended. In some states, the affliction most easily claimed and most difficult to diagnose—chronic pain—accounted for 90% of all physicians' recommendations.[108] It was said that Los Angeles alone had somewhere between 500 and 1000 medical marijuana dispensaries.[109] No one knew how many for sure, but all agreed there were more dispensaries than there were Starbucks coffee shops.[110] Rather than the old and infirm, "[r]emarkably the age distribution of medical marijuana users seem[ed] to mimic that of recreational users in its concentration of young persons."[111]

The 2011 Cole Memorandum

DOJ reiterated and clarified its position in a subsequent memorandum in 2011 drawing a clear distinction between the potential prosecutions of individual patients who require marijuana in the course of medical treatment and "commercial" dispensaries.[112] After noting that several jurisdictions had recently "enacted legislation to authorize multiple large-scale, privately operated industrial marijuana cultivation centers," DOJ stated that

> The Ogden memorandum was never intended to shield such activities from federal enforcement action and prosecution, even where those activities purport to comply with state law. Persons who are in the business of cultivating, selling or distributing marijuana, and those who knowingly facilitate such activities, are in violation of the [CSA] regardless of state law. Consistent with resource constraints and the discretion you may exercise in your district, such persons are subject to federal enforcement action, including potential prosecution.[113]

The surge in enforcement activity proximate to the release of the 2011 Cole Memorandum[114] caught unawares many of those who considered the Ogden Memorandum a green light for marijuana entrepreneurship.[115]

The 2013 Cole Memorandum

The Obama Administration's official response to the Colorado and Washington initiatives was provided on August 29, 2013, when Deputy Attorney General James M. Cole sent a memorandum to all U.S. Attorneys intended to guide the "exercise of investigative and prosecutorial discretion" when it comes to civil and criminal enforcement of the federal Controlled Substances Act within all states, including those that have legalized marijuana for medicinal or recreational use.[116] The memorandum expresses DOJ's position that, although marijuana is a dangerous drug that remains illegal under federal law, the federal government will not pursue legal challenges against jurisdictions that authorize marijuana in some fashion, assuming those state and local governments maintain strict regulatory and enforcement controls on marijuana cultivation, distribution, sale, and possession that limit the risks to "public safety, public health, and other law enforcement interests." This DOJ decision has received both praise[117] and criticism.[118]

The memorandum instructs federal prosecutors to prioritize their "limited investigative and prosecutorial resources to address the most significant [marijuana-related] threats" and identified the following eight activities as those that the federal government wants most to prevent: (1) distributing marijuana to children; (2) revenue from the sale of marijuana going to criminal enterprises, gangs, and cartels; (3) diverting marijuana from states that have legalized its possession to other states that prohibit it; (4) using state-authorized marijuana activity as a pretext for the trafficking of other illegal drugs; (5) using firearms or violent behavior in the cultivation and distribution of marijuana; (6) exacerbating adverse public health and safety consequences due to marijuana use, including driving while under the influence of marijuana; (7) growing marijuana on the nation's public lands; and (8) possessing or using marijuana on federal property.[119] The memorandum advises U.S. Attorneys and federal law enforcement to devote their resources and efforts toward any individual or organization involved in any of these activities, regardless of state law. Furthermore, the memorandum recommends that jurisdictions that have legalized some form of marijuana activity "provide the necessary resources and demonstrate the willingness to enforce their laws and regulations in a manner that ensures they do not undermine federal enforcement priorities."[120] However, the memorandum cautions that, to the extent that state enforcement efforts fail to sufficiently protect against the eight harms listed above, the federal government retains the right to challenge those states' marijuana laws.

Two additional points made in the memorandum are worth highlighting. First, the memorandum acknowledges a change in Administration policy with respect to "large scale, for-profit commercial enterprises" that may ease the concerns of potential state-licensed marijuana distributors and retailers in Colorado and Washington.[121] In previous guidance issued to U.S. Attorneys in states with medical marijuana laws, DOJ had suggested that large-scale marijuana enterprises were more likely to be involved in marijuana trafficking, and thus could be appropriate targets for federal enforcement actions.[122] In the guidance, DOJ directs prosecutors "not to consider the size or commercial nature of a marijuana operation alone as a proxy for assessing whether marijuana trafficking implicates the Department's enforcement priorities ..."[123]

The memorandum suggests that a state with a robust regulatory system for the control of recreational marijuana "is less likely to threaten [] federal priorities ..." than a state that lacks such controls. This statement may inform the long-running debate over the extent to which state marijuana regulatory and licensing laws (as opposed to mere penalty exemptions) conflict with federal law. Some courts have suggested, for example, that whereas a state is generally free to remove state penalties for marijuana use, the more robust a state's licensing and regulatory program, the more likely the law is to be preempted by federal law.[124] The Oregon Supreme Court, for instance, has suggested that states may not "affirmatively authorize" an individual to participate in conduct prohibited by federal law.[125]

The memorandum makes no statements with regard to the application of various federal money laundering and banking laws that have hampered the ability of commercial marijuana establishments to obtain the necessary financing and financial services to establish and grow their businesses.[126]

The 2014 Cole Memorandum

The 2014 Cole memorandum, however, did address banking and money laundering laws.[127] It recited eight priority points listed in the 2013 memorandum and explained that the same considerations should guide the allocation of investigation and prosecution resources to marijuana-related offenses involving financial transactions—money laundering, money transfers, and Bank Secrecy Act transgressions, discussed later in this report.

PREEMPTION

To what extent does the CSA trump or preempt state medical and recreational marijuana laws? The preemption doctrine stands at the threshold of the federal-state marijuana debate. The preemption doctrine is grounded in the Supremacy Clause of Article VI, cl. 2, which states that "[t]he Constitution, and the Laws of the United States which shall be made in Pursuance thereof; and all Treaties made ... under the Authority of the United States, shall be the supreme Law of the Land."[128] The Supremacy Clause, therefore, "elevates" the U.S. Constitution, federal statutes, federal regulations, and treaties[129] above the laws of the states.[130] As a result, where federal and state law are in conflict, the state law is generally preempted, leaving it void and without effect.[131]

Preemption is a matter of Congress's choice when it operates within its constitutionally enumerated powers. In some instances, Congress has exercised its authority so pervasively as to preclude the possibility of state activity within the same legislative field.[132] On the other hand, where Congress prefers the co-existence of state and federal law, state law must give way only when it conflicts with federal law in either of two ways: (1) if it is "physically impossible" to comply with both the state and federal law ("impossibility preemption"); or (2) if the state law "stands as an obstacle to the accomplishment and execution of the full purposes and objectives of Congress" ("obstacle preemption").[133]

What constitutes an obstacle for preemption purposes is a matter "to be informed by examining the federal statute as a whole and identifying its purpose and intended effects."[134] When Congress acts within an area traditionally within the purview of the states, it will be assumed not to have intended to give its words preemptive force unless a contrary purpose is manifestly clear.[135]

The Controlled Substances Act contains an explicit statement of the extent of Congress's preemptive intent. Section 903 provides that

> No provision of this subchapter shall be construed as indicating an intent on the part of the Congress to occupy the field in which that provision operates, including criminal penalties, to the exclusion of any State law on the same subject matter which would otherwise be within the authority of the State, unless there is a positive conflict between that provision of this subchapter and that State law so that the two cannot consistently stand together.[136]

Several state courts have addressed the preemption challenges to state medical marijuana laws with mixed results. For example, appellate courts in Colorado, California, and Michigan have concluded that at least some aspects of the medical marijuana laws in those states survive both impossibility and obstacle preemption analysis. In two instances, they have held that the language in Section 903 evidences an intent to preempt state laws only under impossibility preemption and *not* under obstacle preemption.[137]

The Colorado case, *People v. Crouse*, arose when a defendant, acquitted of cultivation charges on the basis of immunity under the state medical marijuana law, petitioned the trial court to order police to return of the marijuana plants they had seized in connection with his prosecution.[138] The state questioned whether the CSA precluded such an action. The Court of Appeals of Colorado determined that a state marijuana law is only in "positive conflict" with the CSA when it is "physically impossible" to simultaneously comply with the state and federal law. It held that in order to preempt the CSA Section 903 "demands more than that the state law 'stands as an obstacle to the accomplishment and execution' of the federal law.'"[139] Thus, the language of the CSA "cannot be used to preempt a state law under the obstacle preemption doctrine."[140] The decision in *Crouse* adopted[141] the reasoning of *County of San Diego v. San Diego NORML*, a California state court decision that also determined that obstacle preemption should not be applied in determining whether a state marijuana law is preempted by the CSA.[142]

In both instances, however, the court supplied an alternative, obstacle preemption explanation. In *Crouse*, the court noted Section 885(d) of the CSA "carves out a specific exemption for distribution of controlled substances by law enforcement officers."[143] Thus, if the officers returned ("distributed") the marijuana to Crouse they would not be obstructing the CSA but acting in a manner which it authorized.[144]

In *San Diego NORML*, the California law required local governments to issue medical marijuana cards to qualified applicants.[145] In the eyes of the California appellate court, the medical marijuana statute posed no obstacle to the CSA, because "[t]he purpose of the CSA is to combat recreational drug use, not to regulate a state's medical practices."[146]

The Michigan case, *Beek v. City of Wyoming*, involved a Wyoming City property owner and medical marijuana registrant who sought a declarative judgment against a city ordinance which proscribed the use of his property in a manner contrary to federal law including the CSA.[147] Beek argued that the Michigan Medical Marihuana Act (MMMA), which immunized an individual's cultivation of marijuana for medical purposes, invalidated the city ordinance. The City argued that the CSA preempted the MMMA. The Michigan Supreme Court held that the CSA did not preempt the MMMA, but also that the ordinance must yield to the MMMA.[148] As understood by the court, the MMMA escaped impossibility preemption because it was permissive and therefore did not command the performance of an act prohibited by federal law: "impossibility results when state law requires what federal law forbids, or vice versa."[149] The MMMA escaped obstacle preemption because it merely conveyed immunity from the consequences of state law: "the MMMA's limited state-law immunity for [medical marijuana] use does not frustrate the CSA's operation nor refuse its provisions their natural effect, such that its purpose cannot otherwise be accomplished.... [T]his immunity does not purport to alter the CSA's federal criminalization of marijuana, or to interfere with or undermine federal enforcement of that prohibition."[150]

The Oregon Supreme Court understood obstacle preemption a little differently in *Emerald Steel*.[151] State regulators had charged Emerald Steel with disability discrimination for firing an employee for medical marijuana use. The Oregon court concluded, based on its interpretation of U.S. Supreme Court precedent, that "[a]ffirmatively authorizing a use that federal law prohibits stands as an obstacle to the implementation and execution of the full purposes and objectives of the Controlled Substances Act."[152] Thus, "[t]o the extent that [the Oregon statute] affirmatively authorizes the use of medical marijuana, federal law preempts that subsection leaving it without effect."[153]

The continued viability of *Emerald Steel* may be open to question. While the Oregon Supreme Court has not overturned its earlier decision, it has observed in *Willis* that *Emerald Steel*'s "affirmative authorization" obstacle preemption test may have been an overgeneralization: "*Emerald Steel* should not be construed as announcing a stand-alone rule that any state law that can be viewed as 'affirmatively authorizing' what federal law prohibits is preempted. Rather it reflects this court's attempt to apply the federal rule and the logic of the most relevant federal cases to the particular preemption problem that was before it. And particularly where, as here, the issue of whether the statute contains an affirmative authorization is not straightforward, the analysis in *Emerald Steel* cannot operate as a simple stand-in for the more general federal rule."[154]

Finally, in what is one of the few reported statements by a federal court relating to preemption of state marijuana laws, in *In re: Rent-Rite Super Kegs West LTD*,[155] a bankruptcy court noted (in what was clearly dicta) that "conflict preemption is not an issue here. Colorado constitutional amendments for both medical marijuana, and the more recent amendment legalizing marijuana possession and usage generally, both make it clear that their provisions apply to state law only. Absent from either enactment is any effort to impede the enforcement of federal law."[156]

OTHER CONSTITUTIONAL CONSIDERATIONS

Other colorable constitutional issues involving the CSA and state medical or recreational marijuana statutes have arisen on a number of occasions. The Supreme Court resolved one of them when it found that Congress's constitutional authority to regulate interstate and foreign commerce enabled it to craft the CSA so as to categorically outlaw the cultivation and possession of marijuana.[157]

Congress's Commerce Clause authority, however, does not include the power to compel a state legislature to act at its bidding or a state official to enforce its will.[158] From time to time, medical marijuana litigants have invoked this limitation in an effort to shield themselves from the CSA. Because the CSA makes no demands of state legislatures or officials, those efforts have been to no avail.[159] The related Tenth Amendment argument that the CSA intrudes upon those police powers reserved to the states has enjoyed no greater success.[160]

Of course, the purported exercise of an explicit constitutional power such as the Commerce Clause will be defeated, if the exercise is beyond the scope of the asserted power or is contrary to some other explicit or implicit constitutional limitation. In the case of the fundamental rights of the people, the Tenth Amendment, the Ninth Amendment, and the substantive due process components of the Fifth and Fourteenth Amendments all impose limits on the federal or state legislative powers.[161] Here too, litigants generally have been unable to convince the courts that the limitations entitle them to relief. Tenth Amendment reservations with respect to the rights of the people disappear once it is established that the Constitution has expressly delegated a power to the United States, as in the case of the Necessary and Proper Clause and the CSA.[162] A limitation on intrusion upon the rights of the people, however, may flow from the Ninth Amendment and the Due Process Clauses' implicit prohibition on governmental encroachment on a fundamental right.

Fundamental rights are those "deeply rooted in this Nation's history and tradition, and implicit in the concept of ordered liberty, such that neither liberty nor justice would exist if they were sacrificed."[163] The courts have thus far declined to find such a fundamental right in the possession, use, or cultivation of marijuana, even for medicinal purposes.[164]

Due process and equal protection challenges have surfaced both in cases questioning the CSA and those contesting application of the various state marijuana laws. At the federal level, several courts have rejected the suggestion that the government is estopped from enforcing the CSA by virtue of misleading or inconsistent statements in the Ogden Memorandum and elsewhere.[165]

Some of these same cases have rejected the contention that placement of marijuana in Schedule I of the CSA is irrational and consequently constitutes a violation of equal protection.[166]

Municipal zoning or land use ordinances set the stage for most of the state marijuana-related due process cases. State laws vary as to whether municipalities may ban or restrict marijuana-related activities within their jurisdictions.[167] Where they may do so, the regulatory scheme must comply with due process requirements.[168]

End Notes

[1] Section 202(c) of the Controlled Substances Act (21 U.S.C. §812(c), Sch.I(c)(10)).

[2] As of the date of this report, the retail marijuana laws in Alaska and Oregon had been enacted but were not yet operational. The terms "recreational marijuana laws" and "retail marijuana laws" are used interchangeably in this report. Some legislators, advocates, and commentators refer to the laws alternatively as "recreational marijuana laws," "retail marijuana laws," "adult social marijuana laws," or "states' rights marijuana laws." E.g., Malanie, Reid, The Quagmire that Nobody in the Federal Government Wants to Talk About: Marijuana, 44 N.MEX. L.REV. 169, 171 (2014) ("Colorado and Washington have legalized marijuana use for recreational purposes"); Sam Kamin and Eli Wald, Marijuana Lawyers: Outlaws or Crusaders, 91 ORE. L. REV. 869, 878 n.35 (2013)("Many in the

marijuana law reform movement dislike the term 'recreational use' and prefer the phrase 'adult use.' ... 'I don't use the term recreational, I prefer adult social use'"); H.R. 964 (Respect States' and Citizens' Rights Act of 2013); Colorado Retail Marijuana Code, COLO. REV. STAT. ANN. §§12-43.4-101, et seq.

[3] 38 Stat. 785 (1914).

[4] U.S. Const. Art. I, §8, cls. 1, 3, 18; Art. II, §2, cl.2.

[5] H.Rept. 63-23, at 1 (1913)("... [T]he obligations by which [the United States] is bound by virtue of the international opium convention signed at the Hague January 23, 1912, should be sufficient evidence of the necessity for the passage of Federal legislation to control our foreign and interstate traffic in opium, coca leaves, their salts, derivatives, and preparations.... But there is a real and, one might say, even desperate need of Federal legislation to control our foreign and interstate traffic in habit-forming drugs, and to aid both directly and indirectly the States more effectually to enforce their police laws designed to restrict narcotics to legitimate medical channels"), quoted in accord, S.Rept. 63- 258, at 3 (1914).

[6] 50 Stat. 551 (1937).

[7] H.Rept. 75-792 at 1-3. (1937)("The purpose of H.R. 6906 is to employ the Federal taxing power to raise revenue from the marihuana drug traffic and to discourage the widespread use of the drug by smokers and drug addicts.... This bill is modeled upon both the Harrison Narcotics Act and the National Firearms Act, which were designed to accomplish these same general objectives with respect to opium and coca leaves, and firearms, respectively.... Your committee has examined the constitutionality of this bill and is satisfied that it is a valid revenue measure. The law is well settled that a revenue measure will not be held invalid as an attempt to regulate, under the guise of the taxing power, a subject matter reserved to the States under the tenth amendment, if it appears on its face to be a revenue measure and contains no regulatory provisions except those reasonably related to the collection of the revenue.... In addition, certain provisions of the bill may be sustained under the power of Congress to regulate commerce and the power of Congress over the District of Columbia and Territories and possessions of the United States"); see also, S.Rept. 75-900, at 2-3 (1937)("The purpose of H.R. 6906 is to employ the Federal taxing power to raise revenue from the marihuana drug traffic and to discourage the widespread use of the drug by smokers an drug addicts.... This bill is modeled upon both the Harrison Narcotics Act and the National Firearms Act, which were designed to accomplish these same general objectives with respect to opium and coca leaves, and firearms, respectively")(but including no other explicit reference to constitutional authority).

[8] Marihuana Tax Act, §§2-14, 50 Stat. 551-56 (1937).

[9] Id. at §7(e), 50 Stat. 555 (1937)("All provisions of law (including penalties) applicable in respect of the taxes imposed by the Act of December 17, 1914 (38 Stat. 785; U.S.C. 1934 ed. title 26, §§1040-1061, 1383-1391), as amended, shall, insofar as not inconsistent with this Act, be applicable in respect of the taxes imposed by this Act").

[10] The President's Commission on Law Enforcement and Administration of Justice: Task Force on Narcotics and Drug Abuse, Task Force Report: Narcotics and Drug Abuse, 12 (1967).

[11] Marchetti v. United States, 390 U.S. 39, 48 (1968); see also, Grosso v. United States, 390 U.S. 62, 64-6 (1968).

[12] Haynes v. United States, 390 U.S. 85, 100 (1968).

[13] Leahy v. United States, 395 U.S. 6, 29 (1969).

[14] S.Rept. 91-613 (1969). In Gonzales v. Raich, the U.S. Supreme Court ruled that Congress had the constitutional authority under the Commerce Clause to prohibit the wholly intrastate

cultivation or possession of marijuana for medical purposes, despite state laws that permit such activity. 545 U.S. 1, 32-33 (2005); for more information about this decision, see CRS Report RL32844, The Power to Regulate Commerce: Limits on Congressional Power, by Kenneth R. Thomas.

[15] S.Rept. 91-613 at 1-2.

[16] Id. at 10 ("The study shall include, but need not be limited to, the following matters: 1. Identification of existing gaps in our knowledge of marihuana. 2. An intensive examination of the important medical and social aspects of marihuana use. 3. Surveys of the extent and nature of marihuana use. 4. Studies of the pharmacology and effects of marihuana. 5. Studies of the relation of marihuana use to crime and juvenile delinquency. 6. Studies of the relation between marihuana and the use of other drugs").

[17] National Commission on Marihuana and Drug Abuse, Drug Use in America: Problem in Prospective, 458, 466 (2d Rep. 1973).

[18] 21 U.S.C. §§801, et seq.

[19] P.L. 91-513, 84 Stat. 1236 (1970).

[20] 21 U.S.C. §§811-812.

[21] The Attorney General delegated his authority under the CSA to the DEA Administrator pursuant to 21 U.S.C. §871(a); 28 C.F.R. §0.100(b).

[22] For more information about these requirements, see CRS Report RL34635, The Controlled Substances Act: Regulatory Requirements, by Brian T. Yeh.

[2]3 21 U.S.C. §812(b)(1).

[24] 21 U.S.C. §823(f).

[25] See 21 C.F.R. §1306.03 (persons entitled to issue prescriptions).

[26] 21 C.F.R. §1306.04; United States v. Moore, 423 U.S. 122 (1975).

[27] The procedures for these actions are found at 21 U.S.C. §811.

[28] 21 U.S.C. §811(a).

[29] At one point an administrative law judge did recommend rescheduling, but that represents the high water mark for the petition efforts; see, generally, Americans for Safe Access v. DEA, 706 F.3d 438 (D.C. Cir. 2013); and Alliance for Cannabis Therapeutics v. Drug Enforcement Admin., 15 F.3d 1131, 1133 (D.C. 1994), citing, National Organization for the Reform of Marijuana Laws v. Ingersoll, 497 F.2d 654 (D.C. Cir. 1974); National Organization for the Reform of Marijuana Laws v Drug Enforcement Admin., 559 F.2d 735 (D.C. Cir. 1977); National Organization for the Reform of Marijuana Laws v. Dept of Health, Ed. and Welfare, No. 79-1660 (D.C. Cir. Oct. 16, 1980); Alliance for Cannabis Therapeutics v. Drug Enforcement Admin., 930 F.2d 936 (D.C. Cir. 1991).

[30] For a detailed description of the CSA's civil and criminal provisions, see CRS Report RL30722, Drug Offenses: Maximum Fines and Terms of Imprisonment for Violation of the Federal Controlled Substances Act and Related Laws, by Brian T. Yeh.

31 21 U.S.C. §812(c).

32 Very narrow exceptions to the federal prohibition do exist. For example, one may legally use marijuana if participating in a U.S. Federal and Drug Administration-approved study or participating in the Compassionate Investigational New Drug program.

[33] 21 U.S.C. §844(a).

[34] Id

[35] The escalating terms of imprisonment for possession of various amounts of marijuana are as follows: (1) Less than 50 kilograms (110lbs.)/fewer than 50 plants: imprisonment for not more than 5 years, 21 U.S.C. §841(b)(1)(D); (2) Less than 100 kilograms (220lbs) or less than 100 plants: imprisonment for not more than 20 years, 21 U.S.C. §841(b)(1)(C); (3) 100

kilograms (220lbs) or more /100 plants or more: imprisonment for not less than 5 years or more than 40 years, 21 U.S.C. §841(b)(1)(B); (4) 1000 kilograms or more/1000 plants or more: imprisonment for not less than 10 years or more than life, 21 U.S.C. §841(b)(1)(A); (5) Drug kingpin (over 5 or more others and substantial income): imprisonment for not less than 20 years or more than life, 21 U.S.C. §848(a), (c); and (6) Drug kingpin involving (a) 30,000 kilograms or more/30,000 plants or more, or (b) $10 million or more in annual gross receipts: imprisonment for life, 21 U.S.C. §848(b)(2)(emphasis added).

[36] 21 U.S.C. §853 (criminal forfeiture of the proceeds and property derived from a violation as well as property used to facilitate violation); 21 U.S.C. §881 (civil/administrative forfeiture of conveyances and real property used in a violation and the proceeds of a violation and property traceable to the proceeds of a violation).

[37] U.S. CONST. amend. V ("No person shall ... be deprived of ... property, without due process of law ...").

[38] Calero-Toledo v. Pearson Yacht Leasing Co, 416 U.S. 663, 683-90 (1974)(confiscation of a yacht upon which those to whom it was leased smoke marijuana, because the owners failed to show that they had done all they possibly could to avoid the illegal use of their property). In controlled substances cases, there is a limited statutory innocent owner defense if the owner of an interest in the property can show by a preponderance of the evidence that either he "(i) did not know of the conduct giving rise to the forfeiture; or (ii) upon learning of the conduct giving rise to the forfeiture, did all that reasonably could be expected under the circumstances to terminate such use of the property," 18 U.S.C. §983(d).

[39] For a more extensive discussion of forfeiture generally, see CRS Report 97-139, Crime and Forfeiture, by Charles Doyle.

[40] See, e.g., 21 U.S.C. §881(a)(6)(proceeds), and 21 U.S.C. §881(a)(2)(products and equipment used to facilitate the offense).

[41] 21 U.S.C. §881(a)(emphasis added).

[42] 18 U.S.C. §981(b).

[43] 21 U.S.C. §881(e).

[44] 21 U.S.C. §881(e).

[45] See, e.g., U.S. Dep't of Justice, Press Release: Federal Authorities Take Enforcement Actions Against Commercial Marijuana Stores in Orange County Cities of Anaheim and La Habra, August 21, 2012, available at http://www.justice.gov/usao/cac/Pressroom/2012/111.html.

[46] See David Downs, City of Oakland Loses Lawsuit Against Department of Justice; Harborside Forfeiture Case Proceeds, February 15, 2013, EAST BAY EXPRESS, available at http://www.eastbayexpress.com/LegalizationNation/archives/2013/02/15/city-of-oakland-loses-lawsuit-against-department-of-justice-harborside-forfeiture-case-proceeds (describing how a federal magistrate judge dismissed the City of Oakland's lawsuit against Attorney General Eric Holder and U.S. Attorney Melinda Haag, which sought to prevent Haag from seizing the building leased by Harborside Health Center, one of the world's largest medical marijuana dispensaries. The judge held that only the dispensary and its landlords have legal standing to challenge the U.S. government's attempted seizure of the property.).

[47] ALA. CODE §§20-2-1 to 20-2-190; ALASKA STAT. §§11.71.010 to 11.71.900, 17.30.010 to 17.30.900; ARIZ. REV. STAT. ANN. §§36-2501 to 36-2553; ARK. CODE ANN. §§5-64-101 to 5-64-608; CAL. HEALTH and SAFETY CODE §§11000 to 11657; COLO. REV. STAT. ANN. §§18-18-101 to 18-18-605; CONN. GEN. STAT. ANN. §§21a-240 to 21a-283; Del. Code Ann. tit.16 §§4701 to 47696; FLA. STAT. ANN. §§893.01 to 893.165; GA. CODE §§16-13-20 to 16-13-65; HAWAII REV. STAT. §§329-1 to 329-128; IDAHO CODE §§37-2701 to 37-2751; 720 ILL. COMP. STAT. ANN. §§570/100 to 570/603; IND.

CODE ANN. §§35-48-1-1 to 35-48-7-15; IOWA CODE ANN. §§124.101 to 124.602; KAN. STAT. ANN. §§65 41-1 to 65-4166; KY. REV. STAT. ANN. §§218A.010 to 218A.993; LA. REV. STAT. ANN. §§40:961 to 40:995; ME. REV. STAT. ANN. tit.17-A §§1101 to 1118; MD. CODE ANN. Crim. Law §§5-101 to 5-1101; MASS. GEN. LAWS ANN. ch. 94C §§1 to 48; Mich. Comp. Laws Ann. §§333.7101 to 333.7545; MINN. STAT. ANN. §§152.01 to 152.20; MISS. CODE ANN. §§41-29-101 to 41-29-185; MO. ANN. STAT. §§195.010 to 195.320; MONT. CODE ANN. §§50-32-101 to 50-32-405; NEB. REV. STAT. §§28-401 to 28-457; NEV. REV. STAT. §§453.011 to 453.740; N.H. REV. STAT. ANN. §§318-B:1 to 318-E:1; N.J. STAT. ANN. §§2C:35-1 to 2C:35-24, 2c:36-1 to 2C:36-10, 24:21-1 to 24-21-54; N.MEX. STAT. ANN. §§30 31-1 to 30-31-41; N.Y. PUBLIC HEALTH LAW §§3300 to 3396; N.C. GEN. STAT. §§90-86 to 90-113.8; N.D. CENT. CODE §§19-03.1-01to 19-03.1-46; OHIO REV. CODE ANN. §§3719.01 to 3719.99; OKLA. STAT. ANN. tit.63 §§2-101 to 2-610; ORE. REV. STAT. §§475.005 to 475.295, 475.940 to 475.999; 35 PA. STAT. ANN. §§780-101 to780-144; R.I. GEN. LAWS §§21-28-1.01 to 21-28-6.02; S.C. CODE ANN. §§44-53-110 to 44-53-590; S.D. COD. LAWS §§34-20B-1 to 34-20B-114; TENN. CODE ANN. §§39-17-401 to 39-17-434, 53-11-301 to 53-11-452; TEX. HEALTH and SAFETY CODE ANN. §§481.001 to 481.005; UTAH CODE ANN. §§58-37-1 to 58-37-21; VA. CODE §§54.1-3400 to 54.1-3472; WASH. REV. CODE ANN. §§69.50.101 to 69.50.609; W.VA. CODE ANN. §§60A-1-101 to 60A-6-605; WIS. STAT. ANN. §§961.001 to 961.62; WYO. STAT. §§35-7-1001 to 35-7-1062. Vermont has a Regulated Drugs Act that roughly corresponds to the Controlled Substances Act, VT. STAT. ANN. tit.18 §§4201 to 4254.

[48] E.g., ALASKA STAT. §§11.71.190, 11.71.060, 12.55.135(j) (max. fine $500/less than 1 oz.); CAL. HEALTH and SAFETY CODE §11357(b) (max. fine $100/28.5 grams or less); CONN. GEN. STAT. ANN. §21a-279a (max. fine $150/ less than .5 oz.); ME. REV. STAT. ANN. tit. 22 §2383[1][A](max. fine $600/1.25 oz. or less); MASS. GEN. LAWS ANN. ch. 94C §32L (max. fine $100/1 oz. or less); MINN. STAT. ANN. §§152.027[subd.4(a)], 152.01 [subd. 16] (max fine $200/42.5 grams or less); MISS. CODE ANN. §41-29-139(c)(2)(A); NEB. REV. STAT. §28-416(13)(a) (max. fine $300/1 oz. or less); NEV. REV. STAT. §453.336[4](max. fine $600/1 oz. or less); N.Y. PENAL LAW §130.35; N.C. GEN. STAT. §§90-95(d)(4)(maxs. $200 fine—10 days imprisonment/.5 oz. or less); OHIO REV. CODE ANN. §§2925.11(C)(3), 2929.28(A)(2)(a)(v)(max. fine $150/100 grams or less); ORE. REV. STAT. §475.864(3)(max. fine $650/1 oz. or less); R.I. GEN. LAWS §21-28- 4.01(c)(2)(iii)(max. fine $150/1 oz. or less); VT. STAT. ANN. tit.18 §4230a (max. fine $200/1 oz. or less).

[49] D.C. CODE §48-901.01(a)(1). There is some uncertainty about whether a provision of the 2015 Consolidated Appropriations Act, P.L. 113-235, prohibits the implementation of the measure during FY2015. See CRS Legal Sidebar WSLG1182, The Antideficiency Act as an Impediment to D.C.'s Marijuana Legalization Initiative?, by Brian T. Yeh.

[50] ALASKA STAT. §§17.37.010 to 17.37.080; ARIZ. REV. STAT. ANN. §§36-2801 to 36-2819; CAL. HEALTH and SAFETY CODE §§11362.5 to 11362.9; COLO. REV. STAT. ANN. §§12-43.3-101 to 12-43.3-1102; CONN. GEN. STAT. ANN. §§21a408 to 21a-408q; DEL. CODE ANN. tit.16 §§4901A to 4926A; D.C. CODE §§7-1671.01 to 7-1671.13; HAWAII REV. STAT. §329-121 to 329-128; 410 ILL. COMP. STAT. ANN. §§130/10 to 130/140; ME. REV. STAT. ANN. tit. 22 §§2421 to 2430-B; MD. CODE ANN. HEALTH-GEN. §§13-3301 to 13-3316; MASS. GEN. LAWS ANN. ch. 94C App. §§1-1 to 1-17; MICH. COMP. LAWS ANN. §§333.26421 to 333.26430; MONT. CODE ANN. §50-46-301 to 50-46-344; NEV. REV. STAT. §§453A.010 to 453A.810; MINN. STAT. §§125.22

to 152.37; N.H. REV. STAT. ANN. §§126-X:1 to 126-X:11; N.J. STAT. ANN. §§24:61-1 to 24:61-16; N.MEX. STAT. ANN. §§26-2B-1 to 26-2B-7; ORE. REV. STAT. §§475.300 to 475.346; R.I. GEN. LAWS §21-28.6-1 to 21-28.6-13; N.Y. PUB. HEALTH §§3360 to 3369-E.; VT. STAT. ANN. tit.18 §§4471 to 4474l; WASH. REV. CODE ANN. §69-51A.005 to 69-51A.903. The Supreme Court in Oakland Cannabis Buyers' Cooperative held that the federal Controlled Substances Act does not contain an implicit medical marijuana exception, United States v. Oakland Cannabis Buyers' Cooperative, 532 U.S. 483, 495 (2001).

[51] COLO. REV. STAT. ANN. §§12-43.3-101 to 12-43.3-1102; WASH. REV. CODE ANN. §§69-50.325 to 69-50.369.

[52] ALASKA STAT. §§17.38.010 to 17.38.900; 43.61.010 to 43.61.030; Oregon Ballot Measure 91, Control, Regulation, and Taxation of Marijuana and Industrial Hemp Act (hereinafter Oregon Ballot Measure 91).

[53] 309 F.3d 629 (9th Cir. 2002).

[54] Id. at 632.

[55] 21 §823(f)("The Attorney General shall register practitioners (including pharmacies ...) to dispense ... controlled substances.... The Attorney General may deny an application for such registration ... [in] the public interest. In determining the public interest, the following factors shall be considered: ... (4) Compliance with applicable State, Federal, or local laws relating to controlled substances....").

[56] Id. at 636 (internal citations omitted).

[57] Id. (emphasis in the original).

[58] Id. at 636-39.

[59] ALASKA STAT. §§17.37.010 to 17.37.080; ARIZ. REV. STAT. ANN. §§36-2801 to 36-2819; CAL. HEALTH and SAFETY CODE §§11362.5 to 11362.9; CONN. GEN. STAT. ANN. §§21a-408 to 21a-408q; COLO. REV. STAT. ANN. §§12-43.3-101 to 12-43.3-1102; DEL. CODE ANN. tit.16 §§4901A to 4926A; D.C. CODE §§7-1671.01 to 7-1671.13; HAWAII REV. STAT. §§329-121 to 329-128; 410 ILL. COMP. STAT. ANN. §§130/10 to 130/140; MD. CODE ANN. HEALTH-GEN. §§13-3301 to 13-3316; ME. REV. STAT. ANN. tit. 22 §§2421 to 2430-B; MASS. GEN. LAWS ANN. ch. 94C App. §§1-1 to 1-17; MICH. COMP. LAWS ANN. §§333.26421 to 333.26430; MINN. STAT. §§125.22 to 152.37; MONT. CODE ANN. §§50-46-301 to 50-46-344; NEV. REV. STAT. §§453A.010 to 453A.810; N.H. REV. STAT. ANN. §§126-X:1 to 126-X:11; N.J. STAT. ANN. §§24:6I-1 to 24:6I-16; N.MEX. STAT. ANN. §§26-2B-1 to 26-2B-7; N.Y. PUB. HEALTH §§3360 to 3369-E.; ORE. REV. STAT. §§475.300 to 475.346; R.I. GEN. LAWS §§21-28.6-1 to 21-28.6-13; VT. STAT. ANN. tit.18 §§4471 to 4474l; WASH. REV. CODE ANN. §§69-51A.005 to 69-51A.903.

[60] ALASKA STAT. §17.37.030; ARIZ. REV. STAT. ANN. §36-2811; CAL. HEALTH and SAFETY CODE §§11362.71(e), 11362.765, 11362.775; CONN. GEN. STAT. ANN. §§21a-408a to 21a-408c; DEL. CODE ANN. tit.16 §4903A; D.C. CODE §7-1671.02; HAWAII REV. STAT. §329-122; 410 ILL. COMP. STAT. ANN. §130/25; MD. CODE ANN. HEALTH-GEN. §13- 3313; ME. REV. STAT. ANN. tit. 22 §§2423-A to 2423-D; MASS. GEN. LAWS ANN. ch. 94C App. §§1-4, 1-5; MICH. COMP. LAWS ANN. §333.26424; MINN. STAT. §152.32; MONT. CODE ANN. §50-46-319; NEV. REV. STAT. §453A.310; N.H. REV. STAT. ANN. §126-X:2; N.J. STAT. ANN. §24:6I-6; N.MEX. STAT. ANN. §26-2B-4; N.Y. PUB. HEALTH §3369; ORE. REV. STAT. §§475.316, 475.319; R.I. GEN. LAWS §21-28.6-8; VT. STAT. ANN. tit.18 §4474b; WASH. REV. CODE ANN. §69-51A.030.

61 ARIZ. REV. STAT. ANN. §36-2801[3].

62 E.g., DEL. CODE ANN. tit. 16 §4902A(3)[b](“... severe, debilitating pain, that has not responded to previously prescribed medication or surgical measures for more than 3 months or for which other treatment options produced serious side effects....”).

63 E.g., CONN. GEN. STAT. ANN. §21a-408(10); D.C. CODE §7-1671.01(19); MICH. COMP. LAWS ANN. §333.264246(a)(6); MONT. CODE ANN. §50-46-307(1)(d); N.H. REV. STAT. ANN. §126-X:1[X], [XVI]; N.J. STAT. ANN. §24:6I-3; N.MEX. STAT. ANN. §26-2B-3 [G]; R.I. GEN. LAWS §21-28.6-3(10); VT. STAT. ANN. tit.18 §4472(12); but see NEV. REV. STAT. §453A.364 (recognition of nonresident cards).

64 E.g., ALASKA STAT. §17.37.040(a)(4)(1 oz.); DEL. CODE ANN. tit.16 §4903A(a)(6 oz.); D.C. CODE §7-1671.03(a)(2 oz.); 410 ILL. COMP. STAT. ANN. §130/10(a)(1), 130/25(a)(2.5 oz.); ME. REV. STAT. ANN. tit. 22 §§2423-A[1][A](2.5 oz.); MICH. COMP. LAWS ANN. §333.26424(2.5 oz.); MONT. CODE ANN. §50-46-319 (1 oz.); NEV. REV. STAT. §453A.200 (1 oz.); N.H. REV. STAT. ANN. §126-X:2[I](2 oz.); ORE. REV. STAT. §475.320 (24 oz.); R.I. GEN. LAWS §21- 28.6-4 (2.5 oz.).

65 E.g., ALASKA STAT. §17.37.040(a)(2); CONN. GEN. STAT. ANN. §21a-408a(b)(2); DEL. CODE ANN. tit.16 §4904A(3); D.C. CODE §7-1671.03; 410 ILL. COMP. STAT. ANN. §130/30(3)(F); MICH. COMP. LAWS ANN. §333.26427(b)(3)(B); N.H. REV. STAT. ANN. §126-X:3[II](c); N.MEX. STAT. ANN. §26-2B-5[A](3)(d); ORE. REV. STAT. §§475.316(1)(b).

66 E.g., ALASKA STAT. §17.37.010(e); ARIZ. REV. STAT. ANN. §36-2804.02; CONN. GEN. STAT. ANN. §21a-408b; DEL. CODE ANN. tit.16 §4909A; 410 ILL. COMP. STAT. ANN. §130/55; ME. REV. STAT. ANN. tit. 22 §§2425; MASS. GEN. LAWS ANN. ch. 94C App. §1-1; MONT. CODE ANN. §50-46-308; NEV. REV. STAT. §453A.210; N.H. REV. STAT. ANN. §126-X:4; N.J. STAT. ANN. §24:6I-4; N.MEX. STAT. ANN. §26-2B-7; ORE. REV. STAT. §§475.309, 475.312; R.I. GEN. LAWS §21-28.6-4; VT. STAT. ANN. tit.18 §4474.

67 E.g., ARIZ. REV. STAT. ANN. §36-2811; CAL. HEALTH and SAFETY CODE §§11362.77, 11362.775; CONN. GEN. STAT. ANN. §21a-408b; DEL. CODE ANN. tit.16 §4903A; 410 ILL. COMP. STAT. ANN. §130/25; MASS. GEN. LAWS ANN. ch. 94C App. §§1-4, 1-5; MICH. COMP. LAWS ANN. §333.26424; MONT. CODE ANN. §50-46-319; NEV. REV. STAT. §453A.200; N.H. REV. STAT. ANN. §126-X:2; N.J. STAT. ANN. §24:6I-6; N.MEX. STAT. ANN. §26-2B-4; ORE. REV. STAT. §§475.316, 475.319; R.I. GEN. LAWS §21-28.6-8; VT. STAT. ANN. tit.18 §4474b.

68 E.g., ALASKA STAT. §17.37.030; HAWAII REV. STAT. §329-122; MICH. COMP. LAWS ANN. §333.26424; ORE. REV. STAT. §§475.316, 475.319; R.I. GEN. LAWS §21-28.6-8.

69 E.g., ARIZ. REV. STAT. ANN. §36-2804; CAL. HEALTH and SAFETY CODE §11362.8; CONN. GEN. STAT. ANN. §21a-408h; DEL. CODE ANN. tit.16 §4914A; D.C. CODE §7-1671.06; HAWAII REV. STAT. §329-122; 410 ILL. COMP. STAT. ANN. §§130/85 to 130/130; ME. REV. STAT. ANN. tit. 22 §2428; MASS. GEN. LAWS ANN. ch. 94C App. §§1-9; MONT. CODE ANN. §§50-46-308, 5-46-309; NEV. REV. STAT. §§453A.320 to 453A.344; N.H. REV. STAT. ANN. §126-X:8; N.J. STAT. ANN. §24:6I-7; N.MEX. STAT. ANN. §26-2B-7; ORE. REV. STAT. §475.304; VT. STAT. ANN. tit.18 §4474g.

70 E.g., Washington Initiative 502 §31, amending RCW 69.50.4013 and 2003 c 53 s 334, available at http://sos.wa.gov/ _assets/elections/initiatives/i502.pdf (hereinafter Washington Initiative 502).

71 Id. at §20

72 Id. at §15.

[73] Id. at §21.

[74] Colorado Amendment 64, Amending Colo. Const. Art. XVIII §16(3), available at http://www.colorado.gov/cs/Satellite?blobcol=urldata&blobheader=application/pdf&blobkey=id&blobtable=MungoBlobs&blobwhere= 1251834064719&ssbinary=true (hereinafter Colorado Amendment 64).

[75] Id.

[76] Id.

[77] Oregon Ballot Measure 91 §6.

[78] Id. at §54.

[79] Id. at §56.

[80] ALASKA STAT. §17.38.020.

[81] ALASKA STAT. §17.38.020 and §17.38.030.

[82] Washington Initiative 502 §4.

[83] Id.

[84] Joel Millman, Washington State Sets Pot-Sales Rules, WALL ST. JOURNAL, October 16, 2013.

[85] Washington State Liquor Control Board, Marijuana Licenses, Application Process, Requirements, and Reporting, available at https://lcb.app.box.com/adopted-rules.

[86] See Colorado Dep't of Revenue, Permanent Rules Related to the Colorado Retail Marijuana Code, September 9, 2013, available at https://www.colorado.gov/pacific/sites/default/files/Retail%20Marijuana%20Rules,%20Adopted%20090913,%20Effective%20101513%5B1%5D_0.pdf.

[87] Id.

[88] Id.

[89] ALASKA STAT. §17.38.70.

[90] ALASKA STAT. §17.38.90.

[91] Oregon Ballot Measure 91 §7.

[92] See Colorado Dep't of Revenue, Permanent Rules Related to the Colorado Retail Marijuana Code, September 9, 2013, available at https://www.colorado.gov/pacific/sites/default/files/Retail%20Marijuana%20Rules,%20Adopted%20090913,%20Effective%20101513%5B1%5D_0.pdf.at 20-21.

[93] Washington Initiative 502 §26.

[94] Colorado Legislative Council Staff, Fiscal Impact Statement: Proposition AA, Retail Marijuana Taxes, September 24, 2013, available at http://www.leg.state.co.us/LCS/Initiative% 20Referendum/1314initrefr.nsf/b74b3fc5d676cdc987257ad8005bce6a/e3e37fa33a36873887257b6c0077ac93/$FILE/Retail%20Marijuana%20Taxes_FN.pdf. A provision of the Colorado Constitution may affect the disbursements of marijuana-related tax revenue. See Jack Healy, In Colorado, Marijuana Taxes May Have to Be Passed Back, N.Y. TIMES, April 1, 2015, available at http://www.nytimes.com/2015/04/02/us/colorado-lawmakers-scramble-to-keepmillions-in-marijuana-taxes.html?_r=0.

[95] Oregon Ballot Measure 91 §33.

[96] Id. §44.

[97] ALASKA STAT. §43.61.010.

[98] Colorado Amendment 64 §16(5)(f). See also Dan Frosch, Colorado Localities Make Own Rules Before Final Decision on Marijuana Sales, N.Y. TIMES, June 12, 2013; John Ingold, Colorado Marijuana Stores Likely to be Concentrated in Few Cities, THE DENVER POST, July 25, 2013.

[99] ALASKA STAT. §17.38.110.

[100] Oregon Ballot Measure 91 §58.

[101] See Chelan County Judge Agrees with Attorney General's Opinion, Holds that Local Governments Can Ban Marijuana Businesses, Wash. State Off. of the Attorney Gen. Press Release, Oct. 17, 2014, available at http://www.atg.wa.gov/news/news-releases/chelan-county-judge-agrees-attorney-general-s-opinion-holds-localgovernments-can; Jake Ellison, City/County Bans, Moratoriums, and Zoning Approvals for Marijuana Businesses in Washington, SEATTLE POST INTELLIGENCER, December 12, 2013, available at http://blog.seattlepi.com/marijuana/2013/ 12/12/bans-moratoriums-and-zoning-approvals-for-marijuana-businesses-as-far-as-we-know/#18853101=0& 18413103=0; Gene Johnson, No Welcome Yet for Pot Shops in Many Wash. Cities, SEATTLE POST INTELLIGENCER, January 1, 2014.

[102] United States v. Goodwin, 457 U.S. 368, 380 (1982).

[103] Wayte v. United States, 470 U.S. 598, 607 (1985).

[104] Memorandum for selected U.S. Attorneys from David W. Ogden, Deputy Attorney General, Investigations and Prosecutions in States Authorizing the Medical Use of Marijuana, October 19, 2009 (hereinafter Ogden Memorandum) available at http://www.justice.gov/opa/ documents/medical-marijuana.pdf.

[105] Id. at 1-2.

[106] Id. at 3.

[107] Todd Grabarsky, Conflicting Federal and State Medical Marijuana Policies: A Threat to Cooperative Federalism, 116 W.VA. L. REV. 1, 3 (2013)("While the Ogden Memo reaffirmed the illegality of all forms of medical marijuana at the federal level, it made clear that the federal executive policy with regards to medical marijuana permissible at the state level would be for the most part hands-off."); Karen O'Keefe, State Medical Marijuana Implementation and Federal Policy, 16 J. HEALTH CARE L and POL'Y 39, 51 (2013)("On October 19, 2009, Deputy Attorney General David Ogden issued a memorandum memorializing the new federal policy.... This memo was widely interpreted as meaning that the federal government would not be targeting medical marijuana providers."); Sam Kamin and Eli Wald, Marijuana Lawyers: Outlaws or Crusaders? 91 ORE. L. REV. 869, 881 (2013)("In states that had adopted [Medical Marijuana] provisions, the memo was seen as a green light to the open sale of marijuana."); Alex Kreit, Reflections on Medical Marijuana Prosecutions and the Duty to Seek Justice, 89 DENV. U. L. REV. 1027, 1037 (2012)("The New York Times ran a front-page article about the memo under the headline U.S. Won't Prosecute in States That Allow Medical Marijuana reporting that '[p]eople who use marijuana for medical purposes and those who distribute it to them should not face federal prosecution, provided they act according to state law, the Justice Department said Monday in a directive with far-reaching political and legal implications.'").

[108] Gerald Caplan, Medical Marijuana: A Study of Unintended Consequences, 43 MCGEORGE L. REV. 127, 130, 136-37 (2012)("Statewide, more than 70% of doctors recommendations were written by fewer than 15 physicians in Colorado, and severe or chronic pain, a catchall category, accounted for ninety-four percent of all reported conditions.... [In] Oregon, fewer than ten percent of the roughly 35,000 patients holding cards suffered from cancer, multiple sclcrosis, glaucoma, or the other specific debilitating conditions cited in the legislation. Ninety percent of registered cardholders cited chronic pain as their qualifying debilitating disease. Nevada's percentages are nearly identical. Montana's are slightly lower, with seventy-one percent of all medical marijuana users suffering from chronic pain.").

[109] Alex Kreit, The Federal Response to State Marijuana Legalization: Room for Compromise, 91 ORE. L. REV. 1029, 1036 n.33 (2013).

[110] Id.

[111] Id. at 135.

[112] Memorandum for U.S. Attorneys from James M. Cole, Deputy Attorney General, Guidance Regarding the Ogden Memo in Jurisdictions Seeking to Authorize Marijuana for Medical Use, June 29, 2011 (hereinafter Cole 2011 Memorandum), available at http://www.justice.gov/oip/docs/dag-guidance-2011-for-medical-marijuana-use.pdf.

[113] Id. at 2.

[114] Sam Kamin and Eli Wald, Marijuana Lawyers: Outlaws or Crusaders? 91 ORE. L. REV. 869, 881-83 (2013)("In the fall of 2011, California's four Untied States Attorneys announced that a federal grand jury had returned indictments against several marijuana cooperative owners throughout the state, charging them with violations of the CSA. In addition, the United States Attorneys sent cease and desist letters to both dispensary owners and their landlords, giving them forty-five days to move their operations or else face arrest. In addition to the clear threat of criminal prosecution, this action made clear that the threat of civil enforcement—explicit in the Cole memo—was not an empty one. For a federal government with limited enforcement resources, the specter of civil forfeiture is an incredibly powerful tool. Similar crackdowns have since taken place in Washington state, Colorado, and Montana.").

[115] See, e.g., Montana Caregivers Association, LLC v. United States, 841 F.Supp.2d 1147, 1148 (D.Mont. 2012)("The plaintiffs describe themselves as 'caregivers: growers and distributors of medical marijuana to qualified patients within the State of Montana.' They filed their complaint after federal authorities raided their facilities in March 2011 and seized live marijuana plants, dried marijuana, and related equipment. The plaintiffs claim the raids were unlawful because (1) Montana law allowed them to grow and produce marijuana for medical consumption and (2) the United States Department of Justice represented that they would not actively prosecute medical marijuana caregivers."); United States v. Washington, 887 F.Supp.2d 1077, 1090-91 (D. Mont. 2012)("All of the pending motions to dismiss on estoppel grounds rely on the common underlying principle that the federal government, having stated several times that it would not initiate federal drug prosecutions of sellers or users of medical marijuana acting in compliance with the laws of their respective states, should now be estopped from pursuing this federal prosecution in contradiction of those statements. The most prominent of the federal government's various pronouncements on the topic of medical marijuana is what has become known as the 'Ogden memo.'").

[116] Memorandum for U.S. Attorneys from James M. Cole, Deputy Attorney General, Guidance Regarding Marijuana Enforcement, August 29, 2013 (hereinafter 2013 Cole Memorandum), available at http://www.justice.gov/iso/opa/ resources/3052013829132756857467.pdf.

[117] See, e.g., New York Times Editorial, A Saner Approach on Drug Laws, N.Y. TIMES, September 1, 2013.

[118] See, e.g., Wall Street Journal Editorial, The Beltway Choom Gang, WALL ST. J., September 5, 2013.

[119] 2013 Cole Memorandum, at 1-2.

[120] Id. at 2-3.

[121] Id. at 3.

[122] 2011 Cole Memorandum, at 1-2.

[123] 2013 Cole Memorandum, at 3.

[124] See discussion supra pp. 14-19.

[125] Emerald Steel Fabricators, Inc., v. Bureau of Labor and Indus., 348 Ore. 159, 230 P.3d 518 (2010).

[126] For more information about this topic, see CRS Legal Sidebar WSLG682, Banking Difficulties for State-Legalized Marijuana Dispensaries, by M. Maureen Murphy; see also Reuters, Easier Pot Policy Won't Relieve Dispensaries' Banking Woes, CNBC.com, September 5, 2013, available at http://www.cnbc.com/id/101011966; Serge F. Kovaleski, Banks Say No to Marijuana Money, Legal or Not, N.Y. TIMES, January 11, 2014.

[127] Memorandum for U.S. Attorneys from James M. Cole, Deputy Attorney General, Guidance Regarding Marijuana Related Financial Crimes, February 14, 2014 (hereinafter 2014 Cole Memorandum), available at http://www.justice.gov/usao/wae/news/2014/2014-02-14-FinCin.html.

[128] U.S. CONST., Art. VI, cl. 2.

[129] See discussion of preemptive effect of treaties infra.

[130] Northern States Power Co. v. Minnesota, 447 F.2d 1143, 1145 (8th Cir. 1971).

[131] See, e.g., Mutual Pharmaceutical Co., Inc. v. Bartlett, 133 S.Ct. 2466, 2473 (2013)("Under the Supremacy Clause, from which our pre-emption doctrine is derived, any state law, however clearly within a State's acknowledged power, which interferes with or is contrary to federal law, must yield.").

[132] Arizona v. United States, 132 S.Ct. 2492, 2501 (2012)("[T]he States are precluded from regulating conduct in a field that Congress, acting within its proper authority, has determined must be regulated by its exclusive governance. The intent may be inferred from a framework of regulation so pervasive ... that Congress has left no room for the states to supplement it or where there is a federal interest ... so dominant that the federal system will be assumed to preclude enforcement of state laws on the same subject.").

[133] Hillman v. Maretta, 133 S.Ct. 1943, 1950 (2013).

[134] Arizona v. United States, 132 S.Ct. at 2501.

[135] Hillman v. Maretta, 133 S.Ct. 1943, 1950 (2013).

[136] 21 U.S.C. §903.

[137] See, e.g., County of San Diego v. San Diego NORML, 165 Cal.App. 4th 798 (2008)(holding that a state law conflicts with the CSA only where it is impossible to comply with both the state and federal law).

[138] 2013 Colo.App. LEXIS 1971 (December 19, 2013).

[139] Id. at *4.

[140] Id. at *11.

[141] Id. at *4 ("We consider County of San Diego well reasoned and follow it here.")

[142] Cnty. of San Diego v. San Diego NORML, 165 Cal.App. 4th 798 (2008)

[143] 2013 Colo.App. LEXIS 1971 at *4.

[144] Id. at *5.

[145] Cnty. of San Diego v. San Diego NORML, 165 Cal.App.4th at 808.

[146] Id. at 826. The court also found that the California law was not vulnerable to impossibility preemption since the CSA did not outlaw the issuance of the medical marijuana cards that the California law required. Thus, it was not impossible for an individual to honor both the CSA and the California card law. Id. at 819-21.

[147] 495 Mich. 1, 24-25 (Mich. 2014).

[148] Id. at 24.

[149] Id. at 12.

[150] Id. at 14-15.

[151] Emerald Steel Fabricators, Inc. v. Bureau of Labor and Indus., 230 P.3d 518 (2010).

[152] Id. at 529 ("To be sure, state law does not prevent the federal government from enforcing its marijuana laws against medical marijuana users in Oregon if the federal government chooses to do so. But the state law at issue in Michigan Canners did not prevent the federal government from seeking injunctive and other relief to enforce the federal prohibition in that case. Rather, state law stood as an obstacle to the enforcement of federal law in Michigan Canners because state law affirmatively authorized the very conduct that federal law prohibited, as it does in this case"), citing, Michigan Canners and Freezers Assoc. v. Agricultural Marketing and Bargaining Bd., 467 U.S. 461, 478 (1984).

[153] Id. at 529.

[154] Willis v. Winters, 253 P.3d 1058, 1064 n.6 (2011). In Willis, the court held that the federal statute that outlawed firearm possession by a user of controlled substances did not preempt the Oregon statute that authorizes sheriffs to issue "concealed carry" permits to otherwise qualified applications who were users of medical marijuana. Id. at 1065- 66.

[155] In re: Rent-Rite Super Kegs West Ltd., 484 B.R. 799 (December 19, 2012). Whether the debtor was engaged in criminal activity was an issue in the case because "a federal court cannot be asked to enforce the protections of the Bankruptcy Code in aid of a Debtor whose activities constitute a continuing federal crime." Id. at 805.

[156] Id. at 805 ("The fact that there is a difference in legislative philosophy creates no conflict that requires an analysis of federal preemption under the Supremacy Clause."). Part of the confusion over the proper application of obstacle preemption to state marijuana laws may stem from an apparent disagreement over the nature of the obstacle that is required to trigger preemption. As previously noted, the Supreme Court has held that a state law is preempted when it "stands as an obstacle to the accomplishment and execution of the full purposes and objectives of Congress." Hillman v. Maretta, 133 S.Ct. at 1950 (emphasis added). Most courts that have rejected preemption challenges to state medical marijuana laws have interpreted "the full purposes and objectives of Congress" in relation to the federal government's ability to enforce federal law. As such, these courts have generally held that because the state law does not create a shield or otherwise immunize state residents from federal criminal prosecutions, the law does not constitute an obstacle to "the enforcement of federal law." To the contrary, the Oregon Supreme Court reasoned that the fact that the state law in no way inhibited federal prosecutions did not mean that the law did not otherwise create an obstacle to the Congress's chief objective in enacting the CSA; that of curtailing drug use. Emerald Steel Fabricators, Inc. v. Bureau of Labor Indus., 230 P.3d at 529.

[157] Gonzales v. Raich, 545 U.S. 1, 5, 22 (2005)(The question presented in this case is whether the power vested in Congress by Article I, §8, of the Constitution, '[t]o make all Laws which shall be necessary and proper for carrying into Execution' its authority to 'regulate Commerce with foreign Nations, and among the several States' includes the power to prohibit the local cultivation and use of marijuana in compliance with California law.... Given the enforcement difficulties that attend distinguishing between marijuana cultivated locally and marijuana grown elsewhere, ... we have no difficulty concluding that Congress had a rational basis for believing that failure to regulate the intrastate manufacture and possession of marijuana would leave a gaping hole in the CSA. Thus, as in Wickard, ... Congress was acting well within its authority to 'make all Laws which shall be necessary and proper' to 'regulate Commerce ... among the several States.'").

[158] New York v. United States, 505 U.S. 144, 161 (1981)("Congress may not commandeer the legislative process of the States by directly compelling them to enact and enforce a regulatory program."). Printz v. United States, 521 U.S. 898, 935 (1997)("The Federal

Government may [not] ... command the States' officers, or those of their political subdivisions, to administer or enforce a federal regulatory program.").

159 United States v. Washington, 887 F.Supp.2d 1077, 1101 (D.Mont. 2012); United States v. Stacy, 696 F.Supp.2d 1141, 1145 (S.D.Cal. 2010); Raich v. Gonzales, 500 F.3d 850, 867 n.17 (9th Cir. 2007).

160 Sacramento Nonprofit Collective v. Holder, 855 F.Supp.2d 1100 (E.D.Cal. 2012)("[I]t is well established under United States Supreme Court authority that if a power is delegated to Congress in the Constitution, the Tenth Amendment expressly disclaims any reservation of that power to the States. Since the power to regulate the intrastate possession, manufacturing, and distribution of marijuana is delegated to Congress through the Commerce Clause, Raich I, 545 U.S. at 15, [the] allegation that the power to regulate marijuana in California was reserved to California through the Tenth Amendment is foreclosed by United States Supreme Court precedent."). Montana Caregivers Association, LLC v. United States, 841 F.Supp.2d 1147, 1149-150 (D.Mont. 2012)(to the same effect).

161 U.S. Const. amend. X (emphasis added)("The powers not delegated to the United States by the Constitution, nor prohibited by it to the States, are reserved to the States respectively, or to the people."); amend. IX ("The enumeration in the Constitution, of certain rights, shall not be construed to deny or disparage others retained by the people."); amend. V ("No person shall ... be deprived of life, liberty, or property without due process of law...."); amend. XIV, §1 ("... No State shall ... deprive any person of life, liberty, or property without due process of law....").

162 Cf., Raich v. Gonzales, 500 F.3d 850, (9th Cir. 2007)("The Supreme Court held in Gonzales v. Raich that Congress acted within the bounds of its Commerce Clause authority when it criminalized the purely intrastate manufacture, distribution, or possession of marijuana in the Controlled Substances Act, See 125 S.Ct. at 2215. Thus, after Gonzales v. Raich, it would seem that there can be no Tenth Amendment violation in this case.").

163 Washington v. Glucksberg, 521 U.S. 702, 721 (1997)(internal citations omitted).

164 Raich v. Gonzales, 500 F.3d at 861-66; United States v. Fry, 787 F.2d 903, 905 (4th Cir. 1986); United States v. Fogarty, 692 F.2d 542, 547 (8th Cir. 1982); Marin Alliance for Medical Marijuana v. Holder, 866 F.Supp.2d 1142, 1156-157 (N.D.Cal. 2011); Kuromiya v. United States, 37 F.Supp.2d 717, 725-27 (E.D.Pa. 1999).

165 United States v. Washington, 887 F.Supp.2d 1077 (D.Mont. 2012)("Estoppel by official misleading statement ... applies where the defendant had a reasonable belief that his conduct was sanctioned by the government. [It] requires the accused to show that (1) an authorized government official, empowered to render the claimed erroneous advice, (2) who has been made aware of all the relevant historical facts, (3) affirmatively told him the proscribed conduct was permissible, (4) that he relied on the false information, and (5) that his reliance was reasonable. The Defendants assert the defense of estoppel by official misleading statement based on the Ogden memo; statements made to the press or to Congress by then-presidential-candidate Barack Obama, his campaign spokesman, his White House spokesman, and United States Attorney General Eric Holder; the characterizations of those statements in news media; the government's entry into the stipulation in Santa Cruz; and statements made to at least one Defendant by Flathead Tribal Police drug investigator Arlen Auld. None of these statements justifies dismissal on a theory of estoppel by official misleading statement."); Marin Alliance for Medical Marijuana v. Holder, 866 F.Supp.2d at 1155-156; Sacramento Nonprofit Collective v. Holder, 855 F.Supp.2d at 1111; United States v. Stacy, 696 F.Supp.2d at1146-148; United States v. Schafer, 625 F.3d 629, 637-38 (9th Cir. 2010).

The Second Circuit has rejected the contention that the Ogden memo constituted a rescheduling of marijuana. United States v. Canori, 737 F.3d 181, 184-85 (2d Cir. 2013).

[166] United States v. Washington, 887 F.Supp.2d at 1102-103 ("The Ninth Circuit squarely rejected a rational basis challenge to the classification of marijuana as a schedule I substance in United States v. Miroyan, 577 F.2d 489, 495 (9th Cir. 1978). Although Fleming argues that since Miroyan, additional studies and changes in state law have called into question the rationality of Congress' policy, there remains sufficient debate regarding the public benefits and potential for harmful consequences of marijuana use to find a rational basis to uphold the continued classification of marijuana as a schedule I controlled substance."); Marin Alliance for Medical Marijuana v. Holder, 866 F.Supp.2d at 1146-147 ("There is no right under the Constitution to have a law go unenforced against you, even if you are the first person against whom it is enforced, and even if you think (or can prove) you are not as culpable as some others who have gone unpunished. The law does not need to be enforced everywhere to be legitimately enforced somewhere")(responding to plaintiffs' equal protection challenge that prosecutors' threatened to take legal action against them as the landlords of marijuana dispensaries' but visited no similar threats upon the landlords of Colorado dispensaries); Sacramento Nonprofit Collective v. Holder, 855 F.Supp.2d at 1109-110 (same equal protection challenge; same result).

[167] Beek v. City of Wyoming, 2014 Mich. LEXIS 194 (Mich. 2014)(Michigan Medical Marihuana Act precludes any absolute municipal ban on cultivating marijuana within city limits); City of Riverside v. Inland Empire Patients Health and Wellness Center, Inc., 300 P.3d 494, 499 (Cal. 2013)(City may use its municipal powers to ban marijuana dispensaries within the city); Giuliani v. Jefferson County Board of County Commissioners, 303 P.3d 131, 135 (Colo.App. 2012)(municipal officials may ban the cultivation or sale of marijuana within the county).

[168] Santa Barbara Patients' Collective Health Coop. v. City of Santa Barbara, 911 F.Supp. 884, 892-93 (C.D.Cal. 2012)(pre-ordinance permit holder enjoyed a vested right to operate a marijuana dispensary that could not be curtailed without due process of law); Conejo Wellness Center, Inc. v. City of Agoura Hills, 214 Cal.App.4th 1534, 1562 (2013) (pre-ordinance dispensary operator had no vested liberty right requiring procedural due process to extinguish).

Related Nova Publication

State Marijuana Legalization: Issues and Effects

Jermaine Stone

ISBN: 978-1-63485-910-3 Publication Date: 2016

An increasing number of states have adopted laws that legalize marijuana for medical or recreational purposes under state law, yet federal penalties remain. In 2012, Colorado and Washington became the first states to legalize marijuana for recreational purposes. In 2013, the Department of Justice (DOJ) updated its marijuana enforcement policy by issuing guidance clarifying federal marijuana enforcement priorities and stating that DOJ may challenge those state marijuana legalization systems that threaten these priorities. This book examines, among other issues, DOJ's efforts to monitor the effects of state marijuana legalization relative to DOJ's 2013 guidance; and factors DOJ field officials reported affecting their marijuana enforcement in selected states with medical marijuana laws.

INDEX

A

abuse, 26, 28, 37, 60, 63, 95, 96, 97, 101
access, 4, 6, 7, 34, 37, 59, 60, 61
accessibility, 30
accommodation, 37
adverse effects, 54
Africa, vii, 1, 3, 64, 90
agencies, 26, 51
Alaska, 94, 100, 102, 103, 104, 105, 113
amphetamines, 58
amyotrophic lateral sclerosis, 101
anabolic steroids, 97
Appropriations Act, 117
Argentina, vii, 1, 2, 3, 31, 74
arrest, 11, 13, 27, 33, 78, 122
assessment, 35, 38, 39, 40, 41
assets, 79, 119
Attorney General, 47, 83, 99, 100, 106, 107, 115, 116, 118, 121, 122, 123, 125
Australia, vii, 1, 2, 32, 33, 34, 37, 39, 41, 42, 75, 76
authority(ies), 2, 3, 5, 6, 10, 11, 12, 15, 26, 27, 28, 31, 32, 57, 65, 94, 95, 100, 102, 105, 106, 109, 110, 112, 114, 115, 122, 123, 124, 125
avoidance, 35
awareness, 4, 7, 19, 28, 30, 41

B

bail, 37
ban, 54, 64, 105, 113, 126
Bank Secrecy Act, 109
banking, 94, 108, 109
bankruptcy, 112
benefits, 35, 94, 126
black market, 35
bounds, 125
brain activity, 48
Brazil, vii, 1, 2, 3, 42, 81
businesses, 55, 94, 105, 109, 121

C

cachexia, 101
campaigns, 7, 8
Canada, vii, 1, 3, 58, 59, 61, 88, 89
cannabinoids, 57, 64
cannabis, 2, 3, 4, 5, 6, 7, 8, 9, 11, 12, 13, 14, 15, 16, 17, 18, 32, 33, 34, 35, 36, 37, 38, 39, 40, 41, 46, 47, 48, 49, 50, 51, 52, 54, 58, 59, 60, 61, 62, 64, 65, 68, 70, 76, 77, 84, 87, 89, 90
caregivers, 101, 122
CBC, 89
CBD, 47, 50
challenges, 99, 107, 110, 113, 124
chemical, 16, 44, 54, 90
children, 3, 39, 42, 60, 107

circulation, 18
cities, 17, 18, 105
classification, 43, 126
cocaine, 3, 13, 36, 39, 51, 58, 62, 89
coffee, 3, 15, 16, 17, 70, 106
commerce, 8, 10, 95, 112, 114
commercial, 45, 64, 91, 94, 103, 106, 108, 109
community, 2, 18, 23, 24, 40, 42, 77, 79
compensation, 23, 81, 94
compliance, 4, 5, 26, 28, 102, 106, 122, 124
composition, 28
compounds, 44
conference, 52, 90
conflict, 93, 94, 102, 108, 109, 110, 112, 124
Congress, v, vii, 1, 7, 32, 85, 94, 95, 96, 97, 98, 109, 110, 112, 114, 123, 124, 125, 126
Consolidated Appropriations Act, 117
Constitution, 10, 31, 81, 93, 102, 109, 113, 120, 124, 125, 126
constitutional amendment, 112
constitutional issues, 112
constitutional principles, 43
consumers, 4, 6, 15
consumption, 2, 3, 4, 5, 6, 7, 8, 11, 14, 19, 20, 23, 24, 25, 29, 44, 45, 46, 47, 49, 50, 60, 71, 102, 103, 122
Controlled Substances Act, 39, 40, 78, 79, 80, 93, 94, 96, 99, 107, 110, 111, 113, 115, 117, 118, 125
convention, 114
conviction, 34, 35, 38, 59, 64, 98, 99
cooperation, 5, 25, 26
coordination, 39, 48
Costa Rica, vii, 1, 2, 3, 8, 9, 11, 67, 68
counseling, 41, 51, 52, 53, 63
Court of Appeals, 100, 110
crimes, 2, 43, 57, 62, 75
criminal activity, 10, 124
criminal justice system, 32, 33, 39, 49, 51, 52, 61, 63
criminality, 57
criminals, 15, 49, 60
CSA, 93, 94, 96, 97, 98, 99, 100, 105, 107, 109, 110, 111, 112, 113, 115, 122, 123, 124
cultivation, 5, 6, 9, 10, 12, 13, 20, 33, 34, 35, 36, 41, 51, 58, 75, 93, 98, 99, 101, 103, 104, 105, 106, 107, 110, 111, 112, 113, 115, 124, 126
customers, 94
Czech Republic, vii, 1, 2, 3, 12, 13, 68

D

danger, 27, 31
DEA, 97, 100, 115
decriminalization, vii, 1, 2, 3, 20, 33, 47, 49, 50, 61, 63
defendants, 37
deficiency, 101
DEL, 65, 117, 118, 119
delinquency, 115
Department of Health and Human Services, 97
Department of Justice, 37, 90, 97, 98, 105, 116, 122, 127
depressants, 97
deprivation, 23
derivatives, 5, 41, 59, 114
destruction, 5, 9, 10
detention, 16, 19, 21, 27
deterrence, 105
detoxification, 3, 31
developed countries, 59
directives, 15, 16
disability, 11, 28, 111
discrimination, 111
diseases, 29, 30, 49, 63
dispersion, 50
distilled water, 30
distribution, 5, 9, 10, 49, 50, 61, 62, 93, 96, 98, 99, 102, 103, 104, 106, 107, 110, 125
District of Columbia, 99, 101, 114
doctors, 7, 16, 94, 97, 100, 121
DOJ, 98, 99, 106, 107, 108, 127

draft, 33, 49, 50
drug abuse, 26, 28, 96
drug addict, 8, 13, 18, 19, 21, 28, 29, 43, 62, 114
drug addiction, 8, 13, 19, 29, 62
drug consumption, 3, 44, 45
drug courts, 32
drug dependence, 38
drug education, 36, 38
Drug Enforcement Administration (DEA), 97, 100
drug offense, 2, 32, 33, 34, 36, 37, 38, 48, 52, 98
drug trafficking, 4, 19, 98
drug treatment, 3, 37, 39, 40, 41, 57
drug use, vii, 1, 2, 3, 10, 12, 13, 17, 20, 21, 22, 23, 24, 25, 26, 27, 28, 29, 30, 32, 33, 38, 40, 43, 57, 62, 63, 64, 111, 124
drugs, 1, 2, 3, 4, 5, 8, 9, 10, 11, 12, 13, 14, 15, 16, 17, 18, 19, 20, 22, 31, 32, 33, 35, 36, 37, 38, 39, 40, 41, 42, 43, 44, 45, 46, 47, 48, 50, 51, 52, 53, 57, 59, 61, 62, 63, 64, 70, 71, 75, 76, 77, 78, 80, 81, 83, 84, 85, 86, 89, 90, 95, 97, 106, 107, 114, 115
due process, 98, 112, 113, 116, 125, 126

E

economics, 61
ecstasy, 13, 36, 51
education, 4, 7, 32, 33, 36, 38, 40
educational institutions, 14
election, 59, 60
employers, 94
enforcement, 2, 7, 13, 15, 17, 24, 25, 47, 49, 60, 61, 93, 95, 100, 104, 105, 107, 108, 110, 111, 112, 122, 123, 124, 127
entrepreneurs, 94
entrepreneurship, 107
environments, 29, 63
equipment, 39, 99, 116, 122
evidence, 27, 52, 55, 96, 99, 105, 114, 116
examinations, 21
exclusion, 110
execution, 23, 109, 110, 111, 124
executive branch, 81
exercise, 106, 107, 112
exploitation, 94
exports, 45, 46

F

family support, 29
federal agency, 97
federal authorities, 94, 106, 122
federal government, 97, 100, 107, 121, 122, 124
Federal Government, 113, 125
federal law, 34, 81, 93, 94, 95, 99, 105, 107, 108, 109, 110, 111, 112, 123, 124
federal regulations, 109
Fifth Amendment, 95
financial, 23, 94, 109
firearms, 107, 114
First Amendment, 100
force, 5, 48, 55, 56, 60, 61, 62, 110
foreign law, vii, 1
Fourteenth Amendment, 112
funding, 34, 43
funds, 99, 105

G

general practitioner, 14
Germany, vii, 1, 2, 3, 44, 82
glaucoma, 101, 121
good behavior, 38
governance, 123
governments, 17, 33, 34, 45, 61, 105, 107, 111
grand jury, 122
gravity, 23
growth, 100

guardian, 10
guidance, 106, 108, 122, 127
guidelines, 17, 19, 35, 46, 83, 93
guilt, 40, 98
guilty, 40, 59, 64

H

harm reduction strategies, 33
harmful effects, 4, 7, 33
Harrison Narcotics Act, 95, 114
harvesting, 5, 13
hazards, 44, 95
health, 3, 4, 7, 8, 10, 15, 16, 19, 20, 21, 24, 25, 27, 28, 29, 30, 33, 35, 38, 39, 40, 41, 55, 57, 60, 62, 63, 67, 75, 76, 77, 78, 79, 80, 81, 84, 85, 86, 87, 89, 90, 91, 104, 107, 108
Health and Human Services (HHS), 97
health condition, 29
health effects, 38, 41
health risks, 7
health services, 24, 25, 104
hepatitis c, 101
heroin, 3, 13, 30, 36, 39, 51, 58, 62, 64, 90, 96
high-risk populations, 64
history, 16, 19, 36, 40, 85, 113
human, 16, 44, 101
human immunodeficiency virus, 101

I

identification, 21, 27, 64
illicit drug use, 38, 40
illicit substances, 32, 39
immunity, 94, 100, 101, 110, 111
immunodeficiency, 101
imports, 45, 46, 97
imprisonment, 3, 9, 10, 11, 12, 13, 31, 38, 40, 47, 49, 52, 59, 64, 98, 115, 117
income, 17, 50, 61, 116
individuals, 3, 31, 32, 40, 51, 54, 62, 63, 102, 103, 106
industry, 5, 54, 61, 86, 87
intervention, 32, 33, 38, 41, 42
intimacy, 43, 81
intravenously, 30
Ireland, vii, 1, 3, 61, 62, 63, 89, 90
Israel, vii, 1, 2, 3, 46, 47, 48, 50, 83
issues, vii, 4, 7, 16, 29, 51, 77, 95, 96, 102, 112, 127

J

Judiciary Committee, 96
jurisdiction, 21, 26, 27, 39, 72, 81, 101
Jurisdictions, 122
juvenile delinquency, 115
juveniles, 41

L

labeling, 103, 104
lateral sclerosis, 101
Latin America, 4
law enforcement, 2, 7, 15, 49, 60, 61, 105, 107, 108, 110
laws, vii, 1, 3, 9, 33, 41, 57, 58, 60, 76, 78, 86, 88, 93, 94, 95, 96, 98, 100, 101, 102, 103, 104, 106, 108, 109, 110, 112, 113, 114, 115, 118, 122, 123, 124, 127
laws and regulations, 108
legal issues, vii, 95
legality, 7
legalization, vii, 1, 3, 34, 46, 48, 57, 59, 61, 65, 89, 91, 96, 127
legislation, 3, 12, 32, 33, 34, 35, 36, 37, 38, 40, 51, 55, 56, 58, 59, 60, 61, 62, 68, 75, 76, 77, 78, 79, 80, 84, 85, 86, 87, 90, 95, 97, 99, 107, 114, 121
liberty, 25, 113, 125, 126
life cycle, 103
light, 46, 48, 107, 121
local authorities, 18

local government, 17, 81, 105, 107, 111
low risk, 51, 52, 54
LSD, 14, 36, 39, 58, 96
LTD, 112

M

majority, 4, 6, 93
management, 23, 74
manufacturing, vii, 1, 2, 16, 55, 56, 86, 104, 125
marijuana, vii, 2, 3, 4, 5, 6, 7, 8, 11, 12, 31, 32, 39, 46, 47, 48, 57, 58, 59, 60, 61, 88, 89, 90, 91, 93, 94, 95, 96, 97, 98, 99, 100, 101, 102, 103, 104, 105, 106, 107, 108, 109, 110, 111, 112, 113, 115, 116, 118, 120, 121, 122, 123, 124, 125, 126, 127
marketing, 2, 4, 5
materials, 5, 30
matter, 13, 14, 46, 109, 110, 114
media, 8, 76, 77, 78, 125
medical, vii, 3, 4, 8, 9, 12, 14, 21, 47, 50, 61, 63, 64, 76, 91, 93, 94, 95, 96, 97, 99, 100, 101, 102, 106, 108, 109, 110, 111, 112, 114, 115, 116, 118, 121, 122, 123, 124, 127
medical reason, 47
medication, 119
methadone, 30, 39, 64
methamphetamine, 13, 51
Mexico, vii, 1, 2, 14, 15, 69, 70
microorganisms, 44
Ministry of Education, 6
minors, 2, 10, 11, 17, 60
misuse, 41, 51, 62
money laundering, 108, 109
Montana, 121, 122, 125
moratorium, 56
multiple sclerosis, 57, 101, 121
muscle spasms, 101

N

narcotic, 2, 12, 13, 16, 20, 22, 44, 45, 46, 71
narcotics, vii, 1, 2, 3, 8, 9, 10, 11, 14, 15, 33, 42, 44, 45, 46, 57, 58, 59, 63, 96, 97, 114
Narcotics Act of 1914, 95
national policy, 5
National Strategy, 19, 20
Netherlands, vii, 1, 2, 3, 15, 16, 17, 70
New South Wales, 3, 34, 35, 37, 77
New Zealand, vii, 1, 2, 3, 50, 51, 53, 54, 84, 85
Norway, vii, 1, 2, 3, 57, 87, 88
nuisance, 3, 17, 18

O

Obama Administration, 106, 107
Obama, President Barack, 125
offenders, 2, 18, 19, 32, 33, 37, 39, 40, 41, 42, 46, 47, 49, 51, 52
officials, 95, 105, 112, 126, 127
oil, 37, 41, 47, 50, 51
operating system, 26
operations, 105, 122
opportunities, 2
outpatient, 10

P

pain, 101, 106, 119, 121
Parliament, 34, 52, 54, 64, 75, 77, 88, 89, 90
participants, 45, 77, 85
penalties, 2, 3, 6, 10, 11, 12, 13, 15, 32, 41, 46, 47, 49, 59, 63, 64, 81, 84, 96, 97, 98, 108, 110, 114, 127
permit, 62, 115, 126
pharmaceutical, 5
pharmacology, 115
physicians, 47, 106, 121

PIT, 65
plants, 2, 5, 6, 8, 9, 11, 12, 13, 16, 18, 19, 20, 21, 23, 24, 25, 34, 35, 36, 37, 41, 44, 59, 60, 95, 97, 99, 102, 103, 110, 115, 122
police, 3, 10, 13, 21, 26, 27, 28, 32, 33, 35, 36, 37, 39, 40, 51, 55, 60, 62, 63, 76, 77, 78, 79, 80, 84, 85, 110, 112, 114
policy, 5, 12, 15, 16, 17, 19, 33, 40, 45, 46, 68, 84, 85, 106, 108, 121, 126, 127
possession, vii, 1, 2, 3, 5, 9, 10, 12, 13, 14, 15, 18, 19, 20, 21, 31, 32, 33, 34, 35, 36, 37, 38, 39, 40, 41, 43, 46, 47, 49, 50, 51, 52, 53, 55, 56, 57, 58, 59, 60, 61, 62, 63, 64, 75, 76, 79, 93, 95, 96, 98, 99, 102, 103, 106, 107, 112, 113, 115, 124, 125
precedent, 111, 125
preparation, 9, 10, 43, 86
prevention, 4, 7, 8, 19, 28, 29, 38, 78
principles, 43, 100
producers, 52, 104
production quota, 97
professionals, 14, 30, 47, 50, 76
protection, 20, 28, 113, 126
psychoactive substances, vii, 1, 2, 51, 52, 54, 55, 56
public health, 4, 7, 16, 19, 27, 28, 30, 60, 107, 108
public interest, 45, 48, 52, 118
public safety, 107
public service, 23
punishment, 2, 3, 24, 42, 43, 44, 45, 46

Q

qualifications, 103, 104
quality control, 55
Queensland, 34, 37, 38, 76
questioning, 43, 113

R

rationality, 126
real property, 99, 116
reception, 28, 74
recidivism, 81
recognition, 6, 119
recommendations, iv, 53, 54, 96, 106, 121
recreational, 7, 33, 52, 58, 59, 61, 93, 95, 102, 103, 104, 105, 106, 107, 108, 109, 111, 112, 113, 127
regulations, 1, 39, 45, 51, 55, 56, 59, 61, 62, 97, 102, 104, 108, 109
regulatory framework, 60
regulatory requirements, 43
regulatory system, 52, 108
rehabilitation, 3, 10, 19, 31, 32, 37, 49
relief, 113, 124
requirements, 5, 17, 24, 43, 46, 53, 55, 56, 97, 103, 104, 113, 115
resources, 8, 35, 51, 62, 79, 95, 105, 106, 107, 109, 122
restrictions, 2, 55, 56, 98, 103, 105
retail, vii, 55, 94, 99, 100, 102, 103, 104, 105, 113
retaliation, 100
revenue, 93, 95, 104, 105, 107, 114, 120
rights, 52, 112, 113, 125
risks, 2, 4, 5, 7, 19, 23, 28,29, 30, 44, 51, 52, 54, 63, 64, 107
rules, 2, 13, 15, 16, 17, 56, 103, 104, 120

S

safety, 3, 6, 23, 27, 48, 76, 97, 104, 107, 108
sanctions, 5, 11, 19, 20, 22, 23, 24, 25, 26, 28, 55, 95
SAR, 94
school, 17, 47, 60, 89, 104
sclerosis, 57, 101, 121
scope, 100, 101, 112
security, 25, 45, 76, 94, 97, 103, 104

seizure, 21, 23, 99, 116
Senate, 4, 15, 43, 70, 96
sentencing, 2, 37, 40, 41, 44, 53, 98
service provider, 38
services, 3, 20, 23, 24, 25, 32, 39, 42, 45, 51, 63, 77, 80, 94, 104, 109
side effects, 50, 119
smoking, 30, 32, 35, 36, 38, 39, 41, 52
society, 7, 8, 33, 51, 96
South Africa, vii, 1, 3, 64, 90, 91
stabilization, 58
stakeholders, 7
state, 5, 21, 24, 28, 31, 32, 33, 34, 35, 44, 45, 49, 50, 56, 93, 94, 95, 98, 99, 100, 101, 102, 103, 104, 105, 106, 107, 108, 109, 110, 111, 112, 113, 115, 120, 121, 122, 123, 124, 126, 127
state laws, 106, 110, 115, 123
state legislatures, 112
states, 18, 32, 33, 34, 38, 44, 46, 47, 48, 54, 57, 64, 93, 95, 99, 101, 102, 106, 107, 108, 109, 110, 112, 113, 121, 122, 123, 127
statute of limitations, 22, 48
statutes, 101, 102, 104, 109, 112
statutory authority, 102
storage, 5, 9, 10, 55, 103
structure, 47, 54, 95
substance abuse, 37, 60
Supreme Court, 3, 13, 31, 32, 43, 69, 74, 95, 108, 111, 112, 114, 118, 124, 125
surveillance, 104
symptoms, 57
syndrome, 101

T

Task Force, 114
taxes, 61, 104, 114, 120
teams, 29, 30, 74
territorial, 21, 26, 27, 60, 61, 72, 95
territory, 16, 32, 33, 34
testing, 41, 51, 56
Title I, 96
Title II, 96
tobacco, 33
trade, 15, 16, 45
trafficking, 4, 8, 9, 10, 11, 19, 20, 41, 59, 71, 75, 98, 107, 108
training, 16, 19
tranquilizers, 9
transactions, 104, 109
translation, 68, 70, 72, 73, 74, 82, 83, 84
transport, 9, 10, 43, 45, 102
transportation, 99
treaties, 61, 89, 123
treatment, 2, 3, 8, 10, 15, 16, 19, 20, 21, 22, 23, 24, 28, 29, 30, 31, 32, 33, 35, 37, 38, 40, 41, 49, 51, 53, 57, 63, 64, 80, 85, 97, 101, 106, 119
trial, 45, 110

U

United Nations, 59
United States, 93, 97, 99, 100, 109, 113, 114, 115, 118, 121, 122, 123, 124, 125, 126
urine, 21, 58
Uruguay, vii, 1, 2, 3, 4, 65

V

vehicles, 102
violence, 36, 38
violent behavior, 107
vocational education, 7
vote, 54, 60
voters, 102, 104
vulnerability, 11

W

Wales, 3, 34, 35, 37, 77
Washington, 94, 100, 102, 103, 104, 105, 107, 108, 113, 119, 120, 121, 122, 125, 126, 127

wholesale, 55, 97
workers, 18, 39
working hours, 24

Y

yield, 111, 123
young people, 36, 40, 41